IDEAS OF POWER

IDEAS OF POWER

ERNEST HOLMES

Edited and Collated by
George P. Bendall, L.H.D.

 **DEVORSS** *Publications*

ISBN: 0-87516-650-4
Library of Congress Card Catalogue Number:
92-72853

Printed in the United States of America

DeVorss & Company, Publishers
Box 550
Marina del Rey, CA 90294-0550

Contents

A Word from the Publisher

IDEAS OF POWER makes a third volume in The Holmes Papers series, which over a short time has attracted an enthusiastic response from students of spiritual metaphysics in and out of Ernest Holmes' own Religious Science movement.

What accounts for this popularity? Not only was Ernest Holmes a brilliant metaphysician—arguably the brightest light produced by the New Thought movement to date—but he was also intensely interesting as a person, living his life on the plane of direct experience rather than of doctrine, and of self-acceptance rather than of conventional piety and its concomitant, an undue concern for approval.

The brilliance of Holmes' metaphysics emerges from his *Science of Mind* textbook, possibly the greatest single book in the New Thought tradition. However the *living* Ernest Holmes, ranging among a wealth of ideas "sacred and profane" captured just as he thought and uttered them—in other words, Ernest Holmes *off the record*—is almost nowhere to be found except in these priceless documents lovingly conveyed to us and posterity by Dr. Bendall.

No one alive today knew and worked with Ernest Holmes as intimately as George Bendall did—and few have adhered, in their ministry, as steadfastly as he to the teaching of Ernest Holmes, undiluted, uncompromised, and minus the "updating" and "improvement" that would try to add a cubit to its great stature.* As one who in the course of his daily work sees much of this kind of misguided effort, I can only attest to how the stature of Ernest Holmes and his legacy looms larger with each passing year.

Thank you, Dr. Bendall, for these candid glimpses of greatness as only you know how to serve them up from an unparalleled relationship with a giant still standing tall in our midst.

Arthur Vergara
Editor

As in Volume 2, the texts have been minimally edited to eliminate errors and inaccuracies deriving from the transcription process necessitated by these "live" occasions. Bracketed material that constructs or reconstructs contexts has been used sparingly, and footnotes have been added for the reader's information and interest.

Introduction

FOLLOWING WORLD WAR II, the people of the Free World were seeking a Living, Loving God of Hope and Freedom. In this period, and through the 1960s, the rise of healing religion was responsible for a "Golden Age" of belief. The central theme seemed to be, "Prepare us to live today, not die tomorrow."

The Rev. Billy Graham was preaching worldwide. Dr. Norman Vincent Peale, at New York's Marble Collegiate Church, was acclaimed. The Rev. Robert Russell, an Episcopalian priest, was putting healing back into the Church in Denver. Rabbi Edgar Magnin was emerging as a kindred force in Los Angeles. And Silent Unity was flourishing as never before. Many others, too numerous to identify, were similarly making their contribution.

The catalysts so largely responsible for the surge were two great emissaries of the healing message and practice: Dr. Ernest Holmes, founder of Religious Science, and Dr. William Hornaday, who was addressing thousands weekly at the Wiltern Theater in Los Angeles and later at Founder's Church of Religious Science. (Dr. Holmes had relinquished his Sunday-morning lecturing at the Beverly Theatre to Dr. Gene Emmet Clark so that he could be free to lecture in many different places.)

Dr. Hornaday was helping to establish world recognition of Religious Science by speaking and meeting with world leaders and prominent figures in England, France, Germany, Japan, the Netherlands, Switzerland, and Africa. In the course of his celebrated tours he came to know Carl Jung, Albert Schweitzer, and several heads of state.

It was natural that when Dr. Hornaday was away, Dr. Holmes filled his pulpit and substituted for him in speaking engagements. Dr. Holmes often told me that a man with Dr. Hornaday's abilities and charisma came along once in a lifetime. The respect these two men had for each other established a perfect relationship, both professionally and personally.

The actual numerical membership of Religious Science churches may be small compared with the numbers of those in the "traditional," orthodox churches; however it is my belief that the developing Religious Science movement of the 50s and 60s affected all religions and denominations. In fact, Ernest Holmes said publicly that "the movement of Religious Science may be erased in the sands of time, but the teaching and what it stands for will be in the minds of humanity forever."

Out of a "Golden Age," then, come the talks by Dr. Holmes gathered in this third volume of *The Holmes Papers*. Their focus, different from the previous two, helps to give a rounded picture of the man and his thought. And a bonus here is a talk given by David Fink, M.D., a renowned figure in medical circles at the time (1957), whose words lead into one of Dr. Holmes' most inspired talks.

It has been the custom of most Religious Science churches to close their services and lectures with a general spiritual mind treatment for those who had made written prayer requests and deposited them in a prayer box. Dr. Holmes observed this custom; and wherever possible, this book includes at the end of each chapter these affirmative-prayer meditations.

At such times, Dr. Holmes would often establish, for newcomers and regulars, an idea of why he was offering the treatment/meditation. He expressed it once this way:

If you ever get to that place of stillness—out of it everything comes: the uncreated creativity; the creative possibility of the individual out of the uncreated; the voice that was not spoken, yet is ready to articulate—something new and fresh, a creation that never existed and need never again be. But in the passing movements of our present fancy, the word shall become flesh and dwell among us as long as it ought to and dissolve when it is no longer necessary. "Our little systems have their day; / They have their day and cease to be: / They are but broken lights of Thee, / And Thou, O Lord, art more than they."

You and I as practitioners can throw all of our theories and all of our books and all of our previous prayers out of the window now, because they are evermore *about* it and *about* it and *about* it. They are necessary and they are fine . . . but now that divine moment is come. Emerson said, When it happens, throw out all of your theories, leave them all as Joseph left his coat in the hands of the harlot, and flee—for this is a transcendent moment; this is the moment of a new creation. . . .

GEORGE P. BENDALL

3

CHAPTER 1

The Great Secret of Life

In 1955 a report by Dr. William R. Parker and Elaine St. Johns was published entitled "Prayer Can Change Your Life." This report covered experiments in prayer effectiveness under laboratory conditions studying the physiological evaluations of both Petitionary Prayer on the one hand, and Affirmative Prayer with understanding of our deficiencies on the other.

Dr. Holmes said to me, "George, you had better get with this man, because he has proven scientifically what I have been teaching for 40 years." I did get in touch, and I developed a friendship with Ms. St. Johns and Dr. Parker. Elaine and I used to call Dr. Parker "The first man in the history of the world to put prayer in a test tube and prove it." This was on Dr. Holmes' mind when he spoke at the Wiltern Theatre in 1957 on August 11th, 18th, and 25th.

NOW YOU ARE going to find out why this Thing* is here.

I am not tall like Bill† and George;‡ but sometimes

---

*I.e., "what this Thing is that we believe in."
†William H.D. Hornaday (1910–1992), a close associate of Ernest Holmes and pastor of Founder's Church of Religious Science.
‡George Bendall.

good things come in little packages—although Shake-speare said of Romeo (who was about my size), "a little pot soon boils." And I remember Emerson saying that after having attended a political meeting or one of the old-fashioned revival meetings he would go out in the field, and Nature would seem to say to him, "Why so hot, lit-tle sir?" And I always liked that "little sir," because how little we are when we compare ourselves to What Is!

When George Bendall was giving the announcements, he was very modest saying there was a lecture each Sun-day evening and not saying he is the one who gives it. Now here is a very wonderful speaker. When he came to us months ago, I didn't know him; and I saw this tall and handsome man coming in and I wondered, Could anyone be as good-looking as this and have brains too? What a combination that would be! So I just sat down and thought I would wait and see what makes this guy tick— he *looks* all right—and he completely won my heart and admiration just by being himself: very kind, very sweet, very considerate, very dedicated, very serious in his dedication—but with something I can't live without, and that is a sense of humor. I have believed for many years hell is not a place that is hot—it is a place where no one has any wit and everything is doleful.

It is a great pleasure and privilege for me to speak for Bill and to you. This auditorium is not old to *me*; I spoke in it for ten years many years ago. But isn't it interesting that the older we grow in experience, the younger we become in spirit. That is an experience to me, and I know you feel that way. It is an intelligent person who can fol-low Browning and say, "Grow old along with me; / The best is yet to be, / The last of life for which the first was made. / Our times are in His hand / Who said 'A whole I planned'; / Youth shows but half—trust God, nor be afraid." I think that is a very wonderful attitude toward life.

And so I said to Bill, "I would like to do something different." I am not an orator like George and Bill; I am not good-looking like George (I don't think Bill is too terribly good-looking); I am shorter than Bill is—but I shall make no more concessions. So I said, "I don't care to follow the regular program; I would like to do something different. I would like to give an introduction—four lessons. I don't know how to preach sermons; religion is life, living. God is a presence in your own soul. Emerson said we should not say God *was* but *is*—not God *spake*, but *speaks*: the ever-present Reality.

Now it so happens the Religious Science Church is a thing of destiny. It is based on certain things that I want to talk to you about—and I certainly hope you will come all four times, because these are going to be four lessons in the fundamentals that will prepare everyone for the greatest class in spiritual mind treatment, culture, science, and religion the world has ever known, which is given once a year right here by our church. It is the greatest privilege anyone will ever have to take it; and I know you know that.

So this is sort of an introduction to that. I am interested in teaching. You see, we all believe in God—even the fool does—but not everyone understands certain things that we should know if we are going to come into an understanding of what the modern spiritual and psychological and psychosomatic outlook on life is, and put it all together. I believe everyone in this room should be a practitioner, consciously using a definite principle for a specific purpose. Now he doesn't have to be a *professional* practitioner—I don't mean that—but he should know what he believes, and why and how to use it.

So I chose these topics: first, the Great Secret; then, uniting the visible with the invisible, and how the basic principle of this thing works, and the possibilities you and I have of using it.

Bill said, "I wish you would talk about the discovery of Religious Science," and I said, "I will"; and then as I thought it over, I thought, That is silly. Bill isn't silly all the time; and I thought, That is really kind of a crazy subject, because I never claimed to discover Religious Science. I feel more like the little boy who was new in town and was looking for the post office and met the minister and said, "Could you tell me where the post office is?" And the minister said, "Well, I don't really know; I am new here myself. But," he said, "I *can* tell you how to get to Heaven"; and the little boy said, "The hell you can; you don't even know how to get to the *post office*!" You know, I have no reverence for hell, so I am not afraid to use the word. And there are times when it is a wonderful word.

I have a *great* reverence for children—because they don't know enough not to speak the truth. Jesus said, "Suffer the little children to come unto me, and forbid them not; for of such is the Kingdom of God." I have a feeling if you and I could discover that spontaneous proclamation of the child and couple it with the wisdom of adulthood, we should have much more closely discovered the Secret of Life.

I did not discover the Principle of Religious Science. I *did*, however, make a very great and wonderful contribution, and that is this: I was the first person who didn't think he had to be original. Therefore I was the most original person who ever lived—because I figured Truth does not belong to anyone; it doesn't matter who discovered it or what he believed or when.

Find out that thing that Lowell* called "the thread of the all-sustaining beauty that runs through all and doth all unite." That has been my endeavor for 50 years: to find what it is, out of all this maze and mystery, that finally delivers to you and to me what Moses and Jesus and Socrates and Aristotle and Emerson and Gandhi— all of them—were talking about.

What is our relationship to it? I found that in the Hermetic teaching. Now Hermes is rather a mythological figure, like Adam—and of course there was never any real Adam or real Eve; it is mythology, written to teach a lesson, and is all right. Never forget, the Bible was written by people like we are—some better, some worse; some more intelligent, some less; but *people*. Have no particular reverence for anything other than your own soul and the God that inhabits it. Treat the rest rather lightly but not profanely—but with flexibility; and remember, life is a comedy for him who thinks and a tragedy for him who only feels.

You must be the judge sitting in the judgment seat of your own consciousness, not judging the world but your own relationship to it. No one else can do it—no one can

*James Russell Lowell (1819–1891), American poet and essayist.

live by proxy. I discovered in the Hermetic teaching—
1500 years before Moses, in Egypt—practically everything that is in our Bible. Probably Moses got a lot of this
from the Egyptians. I discovered practically everything
that is in the philosophy of the Greeks—Socrates, Plato,
Plotinus; the great line of thinkers of Greece. It is all back
there, said in a different way; and I don't think that is
strange. And I discovered that every one of them taught
that we are living in a Spiritual Universe *now*. "Beloved,
now are we the Sons of God."

And whether it is Plato or Jesus or Emerson or Buddha
or Socrates or Plotinus or Hermes or any of the old guys
who taught a lot of stuff—and don't be stupefied, awed
by them—they were people like we are; happened once
in a while to speak a truth; and we have to put all these
truths together to find out what we know about God,
man, our own nature, human destiny—that Thing which,
whether we know it or not, we are more interested in
than in anything else in the world. Every man is interested
in his search after something that will make him whole.

Now whether we call it Atman or the Absolute or God
or Jehovah or Our Father Which is in Heaven—what
difference does it make? "A rose by any other name
would smell as sweet." We cannot tell. All of these people have perceived a great Reality—this is the basis of
Religious Science; there is but one Power, one Presence,
one Life, one Mind, one Soul, one Spirit: they have all
taught it—Christian, Pagan, Jew, Gentile; every one of
them has taught it. I have no doubt that it is true. There
is one Life; that Life is God; that Life *is* my life; that Life
is your life; that Life is incarnated in us.

Particularly in Ancient Hindu philosophy—and basic

to our philosophy, the philosophy of Emerson and Troward and modern science—is the thought that we are all in the process of evolution, unfoldment. "Ever as the spiral grew, / He left the old house for the new." "Build thee more stately mansions, O my soul, / While the swift seasons roll. / Leave thy low-vaulted past; / Let each new temple nobler than the last / Shut thee from heaven with a dome more vast, / 'Till thou at last art free." This is the cry of every soul. We are not satisfied with what has been, but only with the eternal unfoldment, the more that is to be—"that every tomorrow shall dawn with a brighter hope, and the sun shall set on the day in which beauty alone existed, and the night shall be filled with peace and the dawn with the glory of a new sunrise, whose golden beams spread themselves across the horizon of our hope to warm the valley of our despair and fertilize and irrigate the planes our our aspirations."

I have never met a single man who could not understand what we teach. People are often saying to me, "People do not understand it." I say, *"Why do they come?"* It is ridiculous. Did you know that the average person in public life and teachers of psychology, and what-have-you, in certain places are all wet?—and I mean around the head. They speak of the average mentality as being 14 years old: they are referring to *their own.* Not to you and to me. I don't believe that.

I have never spoken to an audience who couldn't understand what I was saying, if I understood it myself. But how can we expect, if *we* are confused, to deliver anything but confusion? I was taught in public speaking as a kid by the greatest teacher who ever lived: you can tell anybody anything if you know it yourself; and if they

11

don't seem to get it, *you* are the person you have to take care of.

It is simple enough to understand the philosophy of the ages. It is simple enough to come to believe that, whatever you call It, there is only one Power in the Universe, there is only one Presence, there is only one final Law. It is Good, it is Love; we call it God. It is where we are. We are in It. Since It is present everywhere, It is in us. And It is the same God.

It is easy enough to understand and believe what the great and the good and the wise have taught: God is incarnated in *me*. There is one Life, that Life is God, that Life is my life; therefore in *me* is the Power. Now, *I* am not the Power; but *in* me is the Power—"that sets the stars in their courses and says to the wave, Thus far and no farther." *Within me.* And I didn't put It there. It is not by grace of anything I did. I didn't earn it. I was not intelligent enough to have created myself; and I don't happen to believe that I am intelligent enough to destroy myself. I believe that every person is on the pathway of an eternal progress, forever himself and never less—that we shall go on. I believe there are people beyond us in evolution as we are beyond tadpoles.

Now this isn't anything against us, nor is it complimentary to the tadpole. That is the way it is—from the mind that sleeps in the mineral, waves in the grass, wakes to simple consciousness in the animal, to self-consciousness in man, and God-Consciousness in the upper hierarchies of Heaven. Jesus taught this; Emerson taught it; Plato taught it; the ancient Egyptians taught it. It is the basic principle of ancient Hinduism. It is the very cornerstone, part of it, of science because everybody knows that everything is in a state of evolution. But you and I, I think, believe that evolution is an effect of That which is incarnated in us. There is within us that seed of Perfection, that divine Spark—we theologically call it the Incarnation and that is all right: God in me, as what I am, is myself. We are all linked up, by eternal bonds that cannot be broken, to a Power greater than we are.

Now throughout history there have been people who have demonstrated remarkable spiritual power. It did not come just to the Christian religion. I happen to have been born in the Christian faith. Some of you may have been born to the Synagogue. You don't have to leave it. Some of you may have been born Catholics or Presbyterians. There is nothing wrong with either one. We don't say that Religious Science is something you look at and drop dead. It has much to contribute to every man's religion. It is free of fear. It knows there isn't any hell, in spite of what is going on in an eastern city* describing what it looks like. How far many people have traveled beyond our perspectives! They probably have had more time.

We believe in a straight progression: there is that within me right now which some day will be so much farther along than I am, that what I am now is nothing. It has to be that way. We see right here a variation of that; therefore there is an evidence, there is a witness. "He

---

*May have reference to Sodom: "And Lot journeyed east . . . and moved his tent as far as Sodom. Now the men of Sodom were wicked, great sinners against the Lord." (Gen. 13:11–13)

has not left himself without a witness"; "He will not suffer His holy one to see corruption"; "awake thou that
sleepest and arise from among the dead and Christ shall
give thee life"; "do this according to the pattern shown
thee on the mount." I do not know of any religion that
hasn't taught it.

This is the genius—and it is real genius, not in me but
in us—of Religious Science: we boldly started out and
asked, *"Who said so?"* "The great are great to us because
we are on our knees; let us arise." The only greatness you
will ever find in somebody else is what you project onto
him of what, on an equal level of greatness, you receive
from him. How could it be otherwise? Can water reach
a level higher than its own weight? It cannot.

That is why Emerson said if you go to hear a great man
speak, as you come down the aisle you are giving him his
greatness. You are giving it, because you are understanding it and responding at the same level—or perhaps on a
higher level and also understanding it. *Every* man is great.
"What is so great as man?" "What is man that thou art
mindful of him, or the Son of Man that thou visitest him?
For thou hast made him but a little lower than the angels
and hast crowned him with glory and honor."

You know, I found prayer has been answered throughout the ages; and having been brought up in the Christian faith, I thought of course you pray in the name of
Jesus. Now that is fine. But if you had been a Buddhist,
in a sense it would be in the name of Buddha. The
Ancient Hindus said God cannot have a name, He is
beyond all names. Perhaps it was Jehovah. "Underneath
are the everlasting arms"; beneath are the girders of the
Almighty.

Now if we could see Moses the great lawgiver and Jesus the great revelator of individual value, we would have the Jewish philosophy complete, and one part wouldn't repudiate the other. It is only ignorance and superstition, stupidity, that keeps people from gettng together. How strange it seems!

We shall find that all of them have gotten the same results, and most of them didn't get any results at all. Now why? I have said recently that with the publication of this book which Cherry* Parker and Elaine St. Johns wrote—and they are both good friends of mine—*Prayer Can Change Your Life*, coming out of some psychological and philosophical department in a university, to show the action of prayer—I said to Elaine the other day, "You ought to follow it up with another and make it just a little more metaphysical." They have demonstrated non-denominationally out of a university. It didn't have to come from a Religious Scientist, a Christian Scientist, a Jew, Gentile, Catholic, or Protestant. How wonderful! Truth is beyond all this—It is beyond everything; and "Truth crushed to earth shall rise again." "The immortal years of God are hers, / But error wounded writhes in pain / And dies among her worshippers."

I discovered the common denominator and made it the cornerstone of Religious Science. Now I didn't discover the *Principle*, but the *common denominator*. That is all I ever want said about me. Anybody who thinks he discovered God hasn't yet evolved to a low-grade moron. I discovered the common denominator of religious supplication, prayer, "beseechment," announcement, and

*Nickname of William Parker.

modern psychological and metaphysical treatment or affirmation. And when I discovered it, of course I didn't *make* it—I discovered its relationship to all these things, put them together. This is really the only contribution I made—but it is a terrific one, because it lets down the bars and lets in the light from all these places. How little scenery we see if we only look through this small space! Let's take our hand away from the vision, that the eye may see the world as one vast plane and one boundless reach of sky.

Then, after having discovered this, I found they had *all* announced it—like Jesus saying, "It is done unto you as you believe"; Moses: "Underneath are the everlasting arms"; Moses showing in the teaching that he was taken up into a high mountain and whatever land his eye could see his foot would tread upon—"As thou seeest, that thou be'st." I discovered it in every one of them; and the common denominator is so simple, it is hard to accept it—it is just belief, a feeling, *an acceptance*. That is the way it works in us.

It isn't a supplication. It isn't a crescent, a cross, a crucifix. Now these things are all wonderful—I am not arguing for or against. It is not that. It is a feeling in your own mind, right *in here*. A child may have it; a man of wisdom may possess it. Too often the man of overintellectual capacity has lost it, or, as Wordsworth said, he forgets that "celestial palace whence he came."

There is in you and in me a testimony of our own soul, a witness to our own spirit. Now it is as simple as this. The basic principle of Religious Science is free from superstition; it is free from bigotry; it doesn't think we have learned everything there is to learn; it doesn't say,

"Caesar is dead and Cicero is dead and I have a strange feeling myself!" It isn't that way. There is no snootiness; there is no arrogance.

Somebody said the other day, "What do you think of what I am doing?" and I said, "I don't like your approach to an audience." He said, "Why?" I said, "You refer to your audience as 'you,' and I wouldn't go twice to hear anybody who does that. I wouldn't stay through the first talk. It is 'we': what do 'we' know, how are *you and I* getting along? *That* is the common denominator—otherwise I cannot embrace you in my own thought. How do I know that God is Love unless my arms are around you? I don't." How do I know God is Joy unless I am joyful? How do I know God is Peace unless I am at peace? But there is something in me that *is* at peace.

The common denominator is belief. "As thou seest, that thou be'st." It is so very simple, free of all theology, free of all bigotry, free of all superstition. It doesn't say, "Go to page 10, line 9, so and so." All of these things are good; but as Emerson said, "What are they all in their high conceit / When man in the bush with God may meet?"

That is what prayer and meditation does—puts us in the right contact with the Presence and the Spirit and the Power. Now we are surrounded by, we are immersed in, there is in us, that One Life, that One Law—the One Life that animates everything, the One Law that governs everything. I happen to believe—and it is fundamental to us, and I put it there and said it is the most important thing in all of our philosophy—that we are surrounded by God. God is in us, and it is the same God—the God that is in *you* is the God that is in *me*, and that is how *I*

17

can talk to *you*. I think that is wonderful. And the God in you will respond, and that is how *you* can talk to *me*.

We shall know each other in God, and we shall know God in each other; and as our thought of God reaches out to embrace the Universe, our arms will be around each other. There isn't half enough love. There is too much reserve; there is too much fear of being sentimental, of being misunderstood. Who cares whether or not he is misunderstood! The great and the good and the wise of the ages were misunderstood, else they would not have been great or good or wise.

There is that in you wed to the Universe, soul to Soul, mind to Mind, spirit to Spirit, and It is forevermore holding you in Its embrace—"A Love so infinite, deep, and broad / That men have renamed It and called it God."

There is a Law. The discovery of this Law, this common denominator, on the one hand, and the realization of that divine and common Presence on the other, are the two chief cornerstones of our whole edifice. And when you understand them and coordinate and polarize one with the other, and know what you are doing, you are a practitioner—whether it is professional or not. And I would that each in this vast and wonderful audience would make up his mind that no year shall pass again until he knows.

Let me tell you, there is a secret to life, and we have discovered it. There is a simplicity coordinating all philosophies and religions, and we have discovered it. There is a sweetness and a song and a joy that the light of Heaven itself shall cast its glow on the pathway of our own experience, "for Thou hast made us, Thine we are; and our hearts are restless till they rest in Thee."

Next Sunday I shall talk on the subject of the Use and Power of Faith and try to explain the principle running through all these modern metaphysical movements that makes them effective, and the simplicity of that thing. Our greatest trouble is to believe in that simplicity. Through some strange reason, too many people feel if anything is going to be deep and profound, it must be something no one can understand. Now that is not true. Jesus was the most simple man; he was as profound as Plato. I have studied both all my life.

You and I use the Mind that is God, therefore we do not put any power into our thought. We do not put any power into our treatment. We do not put any power into our faith, any more than you put energy into life. If you and I had to energize energy, where would we get the energy with which to energize energy? It is ridiculous. We may only take it out. But there is a way of doing it effectively. That is what I want to talk about next time, and I hope you will all come.

AFFIRMATIVE-PRAYER MEDITATION

Now we have names here of people who have asked for our help. Let us together know that everyone whose name is in here is known to the divine Intelligence that is in us right now. And we are one with them and the Law of Good that responds to them.

We are recognizing the divine Presence in them and their affairs, and we are affirming that the Presence of God is perfect and active. There is one Life, that Life is God, that Life is their life now. Whatever

19

needs to be changed mentally or physically is changed to comply with the divine Pattern of their own perfection.

We are recognizing God. There is one Presence in them and but one Life, and they are that Life, and that Life is what they are. I am that which Thou art, eternal everlasting Good, and Thou art that which I am—sweet Presence, O sweet and beautiful Presence, inhabitating eternity, and in my soul and in everybody here. Their requests are fulfilled by the Law of Love.

Anyone who has needed help in his circumstances is inspired to do and think and act in that way which will bring wholeness and prosperity and success to every honest and legitimate endeavor.

Now as we silently bless these people, we know this blessing is real, dynamic, and powerful, far-reaching, as eternal as God. We do bless, and our love does surround; and that good will now acting as the Law of Life and the Love of God binds us together, so sweet, so beautiful, so sweet our Love. Now as we turn within, let us silently bless each other. It is so real, it is so immediate, it is so warm. We are embracing each other in love, in fellowship, not forgetting the joy and the laughter and song. "There is ever a song somewhere, my dear; there is ever a song somewhere"—and we shall sing it, and we *do* sing it.

Now may the eternal Spirit which surrounds us glorify Itself in us, because we have opened ourself to Its influx. May the Light of Heaven bathe us in joy and in fulfillment and in love. Amen.

CHAPTER 2

The Use and Power of Faith

THIS IS OUR second lesson in our series of What This Thing Is We Believe In; Why We Believe in It; The Way We Think It Works; and What We Know about Using It. You remember last week we discussed a Principle of Life which is as simple as this: we live in a universal Mind and Spirit. There is one Mind and one Spirit, which is God. Now every time we think, we use this Mind; and Law is Mind in action. As Dr. [John] Haldane, the great biologist, said, the only thing that science has discovered that is creative is mind. Back of mind is consciousness, or thought. "In the beginning was the Word."

Now Religious Science I consider to be the greatest movement of modern times, or I wouldn't be here—and I don't think you would on quite as warm a day as this. The other day I asked someone, "Is this similar to hell?" Now of course, I shouldn't have asked this person; I have no reason to suppose he has ever been there. I think we have *all* been there; and when people ask me if I believe in hell, I say, "*Certainly*: I believe in the hell we are getting out of. There isn't any other."

The Universe does not insult us after it has injured us. We may be certain of that. As Emerson said, "The finite alone has wrought and suffered, the Infinite lies stretched in smiling repose." He said another thing I love: "We see the universe as solid fact, but God sees it as liquid law." That is the Law of Consciousness.

We said that consciousness—thought, something we know; feeling, thinking—is basic to everything and that we are surrounded by a divine and universal Intelligence which receives the impress of our thought and acts upon it creatively. For "Mind is the power that moulds and makes / And man is mind, and ever more he takes / The tool of thought and, shaping what he wills, / Brings forth a thousand joys, a thousand ills. / He thinks in secret and it comes to pass, / Environment is but his looking glass."

There *was* a secret to the miracles of Jesus, and we have discovered it. This "secret" Religious Science, for the first time in the history of the world, lays bare without prejudice. Now other people have known it. We are not better than other people. We are worse than everybody else in the world—but smarter. And that makes us more interesting. I wouldn't swap any one of us for ten of anybody else on earth. Why? Because, knowing nothing, we fear nothing. And that is a wonderful state to be in. Shakespeare said, "Where ignorance is bliss, 'tis folly to be wise." Very profound statement.

We know something that we are not afraid of, and we have not created a new devil to take the place of the old one, which we weren't able to sublimate but just had to dress up and call by a different name. You know, Religious Science is more than a revelation—it is THE revelation of revelations. I was talking to Dr. Barclay Johnson the other day, and I said, "You have built up such a wonderful course." (He is the head of our College. He has put together the greatest courses we have ever had.) I said to him, if I could persuade everyone in this room to take this course we would have a couple of thousand of the most emancipated people in the world; and if they knew what is offered them, they would demand it. And I am talking about *you*.

There is no other place in the world where it is given. There are no other people in the world so free from prejudice. Now I want to talk this morning on faith and the use and power of it, the ever-available law of faith and the measure of the principle of faith, and how it works, how to acquire it, how to use it, and the principle underlying it. That is enough for 13 talks right there. But we have so little time; we have to cover a lot of territory, and I want to begin by explaining something to you that some of you know but that some don't.

Within the last three months a new book* published by Prentice-Hall came on the market, written by two friends of mine, Elaine St. Johns and Dr. "Cherry" Parker of Redlands University, a wonderful man, very spiritual. Remember, one of the accusations laid against Jesus was that he appeared at feasts, turned the water into wine, multiplied the loaves and fishes, raised Lazarus from the dead, brought the boat immediately to the shore, showed them where to get money for their taxes, and resurrected himself from the dead. And they said, "No good thing can

Prayer Can Change Your Life.

come out of Nazareth, because this man has permitted an evil woman, a prostitute, to bathe his feet." She bathed them with her tears; and I wrote: "How wondrous kind his words of love to the penitent kneeling there, / Who bathed his feet in tears of joy and dried them with her golden hair."

Here is a man, the man of the ages, who had one hand in the ever-outstretched hand of God and the other one embracing humanity. You and I will never know, no matter how high-sounding our theories are or how beautiful they sound or what they mean semantically. However, if I say to you, "I love you," you know what I mean; and if you say, "I love you too," I know what you mean; and when we embrace, we know how we feel. The semanticist may not.

That which instinctively rises from the human breast to proclaim the need of the finite heart is an utterance of the feeling of the Universe and may be considered the word of Almighty God. For the only God you and I will ever know is the One we embody. Never forget that.

Now Dr. Cherry Parker tried several years' experiments at Redlands University (nonsectarian in their faith: there would be Jews and Gentiles and Protestants and Catholics; there would be no God who ever heard there was a difference. But don't tell any of the people who haven't found it out but remain in splendid isolation and frozen emotions).

That is a good way to be—until you wake up. "Awake, thou that sleepest, and arise from the dead, and Christ shall give thee life."

Elaine St. Johns is the daughter of Adela Rogers St. Johns, who is like a sister to me and always was to my wife. Now, this* is the account which Elaine wrote based on the experiments of Cherry Parker. (Elaine and my brother Fenwicke are helping me to write a history of our movement. They didn't think I had sense enough to write it. And the funny part of it is, they were right.) This is based on three experiments with prayer. The first one is called Spiritual Psychological Counseling; the next one is called Ordinary Prayer, which all the world prays; and the last experiment is called Prayer Therapy, which Cherry used, and you and I believe in. Now affirmative prayer is what you and I believe in, but remember this: affirmative prayer means an affirmation the mind consciously uses for a definite purpose which it believes is accomplished as much as it can even though it hasn't seen it.

The prayer is uttered by the mind as affirmation and acceptance flowing out of consciousness of feeling and belief and faith, and it is identified with some person, place, or thing. Now he found that in the first category—psychological counseling, spiritual counseling—there were pretty good results, definite results. He found that in what I am going to call *affirmative prayer*, and he called *prayer therapy*, there were exceedingly good results—the best of all. And he found—and I am glad this came out of a university, so no one can criticize people in our field for saying it—that the poorest results came from the ordinary method of prayer as practiced by the world of theology. Now isn't this a knockout!

This is one of the most significant things ever to have happened. Here is a university without the prejudice of

*I.e. *Prayer Can Change Your Life.*

a particular theology (I don't criticize any theologies, because I don't think any of them needs that much attention—and I don't believe in criticizing anyway), and here is what they found impersonally among groups of people—some were ministers, some were doctors, some were this, that, or the other—over a period of two years: that the ordinary prayer that the ordinary person prays—no matter how good he is or how sincere, and no matter what his religion is, Catholic, Jew, Protestant (it is all the same—Jesus said "He is no respecter of persons; He causes His sun to shine and His rain to fall alike on the just and the unjust")—they found that the ordinary prayer got much poorer results than just good, sound psychological counseling. Isn't that terrific?

And they found the highest percentage of results came from what you and I will call *affirmative prayer* through acceptance, belief in consciousness, embodiment in thought. They applied the acceptance *to* something *for* something, identifying *this* with *that*—like saying "This word is for John Smith. As a result of this treatment [or this prayer] there will be a new activity over there. As a result of *this*, that confusion will cease." Now that is what I mean by *identification*.

The prayer has to be made *in here*; it has to be *affirmative*; it must be *accepted*; it must *identify* with something, if something is to happen, which shows we are dealing with Intelligence. Now they found also that the attitudes of forgiveness, of unselfishness, of kindness, of joy, of enthusiasm were salutary. I have made a record called "Enthusiasm Is God's Medicine." Do you know it is now known that at least three-fourths of the illness of continual fatigue, and probably most of it where there is no infection in the physical body, may be directly attributed to a lack of enthusiastic interest in life—? And I can see how that would be.

Did you ever get full of an idea and rush up to some friend and say, "Oh, listen to this," and you go on and say and say it—and then he says, "Oh yeah?" And then you wish you were dead. Your enthusiasm is knocked down; and this is psychological frustration—a lack of just plain enthusiastic interest that makes the kid sing and dance and jump up and down and scream; and you know adults *would*—but as Wordsworth said, experience closes them round until they are encased in a prison wall and they forget that celestial palace whence they came.

Isn't it too bad that people when they grow up won't still scream and holler a little and jump up and down a little and once in a while say something that they have not premeditated—to relieve the tension and let the holier ones be surprised.

Who cares!

If we could only live!

Jesus said, "I have come that you might have life, and that you might have it more abundantly." They discovered this thing in a psychological experimental laboratory in a university, just as they have discovered in another one that which can demonstrate scientifically the ongoingness of the human soul. I am so glad that it came out of a laboratory, so no one can tag it theologically.

Now that is what our work is based on—faith. But what is it? You see, there is something people don't understand: that we are dealing with mental attitudes. They don't know there are definite techniques which we teach in our College—absolutely definite. There isn't a person here who, if he will take the very short time to take that course—because the money isn't as much as you would pay to go to a series of pictures; we are nonprofit . . . if you would only do it; and I expect you will after these four talks. And if you don't, I shall forever lose not faith in humanity but in my ability to convince anybody of anything.

Here you and I have within our reach the greatest good the world has ever known. I saw it unhesitatingly—we have the most perfect teaching, the greatest technique, and the best instruction the world has ever had—to definitely and deliberately show the method and the process that is proven at Duke University and at Redlands now, and that has been the hope and aspiration of all the religious endeavors of the world.

Faith is a mental attitude. It can be consciously, definitely, and deliberately induced. You can learn how to give a scientific, effective spiritual mind treatment so there will be no question about the result for yourself and for others. This is the greatest "experiment"—the greatest experience, the greatest good, and the greatest joy that can come to the human mind.

Faith, then, must deal with a law in Nature or itself be a "nature." Now let me explain this. These talks I am giving are preliminary to the course I want you to take— because I would like these 2000 people here, before the year is over, every one to be a practitioner. You don't have to do it professionally; but you want to practice for yourself and your family. You want betterment. You want greater happiness, more success, better health—and above everything else, the thing that intrigues me: not the "signs following," but *the fact that there is such a Power available*—the ever-available Power of Good. It is the greatest good on earth.

Now faith either *is* the law, or *follows* a law, or is *operated upon by* a law—in my estimation. Let's follow it out. Don't think it is hard to understand. Frequently people say to me, "You shouldn't try to talk in public—nobody knows what you are talking about"; and I say, "That is why I have always had such big audiences." It makes me think of a man we used to have—the most popular speaker we ever had, and the most popular speaker at UCLA. He had peculiar eccentricities, and people who knew the art of public speaking would often come to him and say, "Now if you would learn how to speak, you would be *so* effective." And he said, "I am going to when I get time; but you know, most of my life I have had to make my living speaking, and when I have enough saved up so I can learn how, I am going to do that." So far, he is still speaking.

This thing is so simple. *Faith is a mental attitude*. It isn't a new kind of underwear, or something you eat. *It is the way you think*. Faith is thought moving consciously, definitely, for a specific purpose and—if it is *real* faith—accepting the outcome of the purpose. You know just as much about this as I do. The only difference is that I am not afraid to talk about it in public. But if you knew the experience I had when I first began! Three or four days after I made an engagement to speak, I felt as though somebody was continuously kicking me in the stomach and there was no place to throw it up. It is the most awful feeling. But once I got on the platform, I forgot it. I don't know whether everybody has that or not; but it must be like seasickness.

Does a seed you plant operate upon the soil or does the soil operate upon the seed? I don't know. When they get together, something happens. So Jesus likened faith to a seed. The Word. The Bible says that in the beginning was the Word and everything was made by it, etc. Now faith is either a law in itself or it is operated upon by a law. I personally choose to think of it as being operated on by a law, even though it is a law of faith in itself. I'll tell you why.

I happen to believe that just as we are operated upon by physical forces, such as magnetism, attraction, repulsion, adhesion, cohesion, gravitational force, these are not personal things but they personalize. Now I like to feel that faith is operated upon by a principle—so that I won't feel I have to energize energy; because if I had to energize energy, I wouldn't know where I would get the energy with which to energize energy. This is one of the secrets of Jesus: nonresistance.

He said, "Who, by taking thought, can add one cubit to his stature?" and then turned right around and said, "If you believe, it is done." One explains the other. We do not make things happen; we *permit* them to. We supply the condition under which they may, shall, can, and—I believe—*must*. And I think Jesus announced it when he said, "It is done unto you *as* you believe." I happen to believe that. Therefore *I* believe. Don't accept it because *I* believe it. It will be discussed in the class.

Everything is operated upon by cosmic forces. "The Father seeketh such." "The wind bloweth where it listeth, and no man knoweth from whence it cometh nor whither it goeth, and so is everyone who is born of the kingdom."

"It is done unto you as you believe." I believe that faith acts like a law because it is operated upon by a law.

Haldane,* the great modern thinker and scientist, said that all the laws in the universe operate as though they were intelligence operating mathematically as law. Eddington† said this; Jeans‡ said that we can think of life or God as an infinite Thinker thinking mathematically. That is rather interesting. There is a mathematics to our treatment—it deals with our conscious perception and our psychological reaction to it. When you give a spiritual mind treatment or pray effectively, you are alone with the Great Reality of things. Jesus said, "The Father who seeth in secret will reward you openly."

You are at the center of the Universe—the very center and core of all causation. There is nothing out here that has anything to do with what you are doing—nothing. It is to get away from the appearance, to get away from the judgment and the conviction of fact as it is now experienced to the glorious realization that, as Jesus said, "Out of these stones God can raise up seed unto Abraham"—or, *the Law can work*. Now to me this is the essence of faith.

But only a few people throughout the ages have had that sublime and divine faith, and they stand apart from the multitude and people who say that Jesus was God, and the others are favorites of God, and this one and that one God did more for. Nonsense, and more nonsense,

*J.B.S. Haldane (1892–1964), British scientist.
†Sir Arthur Eddington (1882–1944), English astronomer.
‡Sir James Jeans (1877–1946), English physicist.

and still more nonsense! And when they said it to Jesus, he said—out of the enlightenment of that great mind and heart and soul and intellect—"Why callest thou me good? There is none good save one, which is God." And when they sought by force to make him a ruler, he said *no*: "I have come to bear witness to that truth that makes you free. *I* have nothing to do with it." He said, "It is expedient that I go away that the Spirit within you shall now bear witness to that divine Fact—I have revealed you to yourself; I have shown you the way. Walk ye in it!" That is the very essence of Religious Science.

Destined.

Destined to heal the world—someday, sometime, somewhere, as Browing said: "In God's good time it will arrive, / As birds pursue their trackless paths; / Some way I know not when or how, / In God's good way when God has made / The pile complete . . ." and don't forget it. You and I are in the vanguard of the greatest spiritual movement the world has ever known. And out of your heart and mine and your mind and mine—trained to think, to work—shall come the force and the propulsion and the impulsion—the impulsion of Love and the propulsion of Law—that may heal the world. That is why I am interested in our classes and in our instruction.

Not everyone has that great faith. I didn't have it. But I learned there is a key, there is a secret—not a mystery. There is a way in which any living soul may consciously reproduce the monumental works of those who have that faith; "And greater things than these shall ye do." Faith understood, life understood: that is our whole teaching— to the simple, to the great, to the wise. I would just as soon explain this to the children—they know it. I would just as soon debate it with the greatest philosophers and scientists in the world. And I will never have to leave the platform—never.

The Universe is self-existent, and God comes new and fresh in the perennial springtime of every moment, bursts forth from the timeless infinite into the present incident, carrying with it the wonder, the majesty, and the might and the warmth and color of the Eternal Itself. Such is the nature of our being. Every day is a new beginning. Every day is the world made new.

Faith is a law. Now the next point, then: we talk about the principle—how should we acquire it. You and I know it is wonderful. We say, "If we had faith, if we had faith." Jesus, said, "If you have faith as a grain of mustard seed, you could say to this mountain, Move." Now, after nearly 2000 years, without prejudice, without superstition, without the claim of any special revelation or dogmatism which says, "Look at me and die": if I have made any contribution to this thing, I think I have taken the "miss" out of mystery, the dogma and intolerance and stupidity out of special revelations, and revealed at long last the simplicity of that Thing which has run like a golden thread of beauty through the great religions of the world—what Lowell called "that thread of the all-sustaining Beauty that runs through all and doth all unite."

You and I may sing a hymn of praise this morning to the creative genius of the Universe that at least this much of the blindfold has been removed, so that we are no longer hesitant to say to the least among us, to a beggar —at last having searched a lifetime for the Holy Grail or the chalice of the eternal Giver—"I behold in thee the image of Him who died on the tree." And Jesus said, "Let him who is least be greatest; he who is greatest, let him be least." There is a nonresistance that cannot be resisted, a nonviolence that cannot be violated, a prayer of faith the integrity of which is the nature of the Law of the Universe. And Jesus said, "Heaven and earth shall pass away, but my word shall not until it is fulfilled."

Now I want you to know he was talking about *you;* and *I* am talking about you; and you are listening to that Thing within *yourself* which says *Yes*—and I didn't put It there. It was there when you came in—in a few words of conversation, or the communion of spirit with Spirit as we embrace each other in the love of God or the adoration of God; "and the love of humanity shall be torchlight." Emerson said, "Take this torch and advance and advance on chaos and the night."

Faith can be acquired by conscious, definite, deliberate methods of procedure in your own mind—so simple that a child five years old can understand it; so profound that no philosopher who ever lived can refute it; so demonstrable that no scientific mind can successfully repudiate it; so much a thing of consciousness that it carries all of our psychological reactions into a transcendence; and so human that it bears the message of love to the heart sitting alone in the darkness of human isolation, for all the world is crying for light. There is solace for the hearts longing for love—for the world is dying just for a little bit of love and to be embraced; and people are afraid of it and they misunderstand it. Emerson said, "To be great is to be misunderstood." Over the doorway of consistency I would write, "Thou Fool!" And Jesus had to take a little boy with him—just a little brat who didn't know it couldn't be done, and the man of wisdom who knew that it could. And joining their forces together, God Almighty multiplied the loaves and the fishes.

But of what use are all these things unless we use them? *What good are all these things unless we use them??* We learn things: we learn to dance, that we may dance; we learn to sing, that we may sing; we learn to write, that we may write. *We learn to have faith, that we may demonstrate it.*

The supremacy of spiritual thought-force over all apparent material resistance: I don't know of any joy on earth equal to the joy, the gratification, not of a sense of personal power—that wouldn't do it—but of the sense of the wonder of life and the miracle of life; of the sense of our partnership with the Infinite; of the sense that we may put our feet forth into what seems an apparent void, only to find them placed upon the Rock of the Ages. I do not know of any gratification that can come to the human mind or heart equal to listening in the silence and the independence and the freedom and the aloneness of one's own soul—and then someday looking out, seeing and kissing the object of our desire. What can be more wonderful?

So they proved all these things at a university, way beyond psychological counseling—there is nothing wrong with psychological counseling, I believe in it—way beyond the average prayer. There is nothing wrong with the simple, sweet, and sincere prayer. But we are talking about science and sense—pragmatic, practical things that are right down to earth: what will produce two ears of corn instead of one, how to make the hen lay more eggs or the cow give more milk; it is as practical as that.

We are going to take the time to pray. If we believe

there is Something that responds, don't we want to know the best method? Don't we want to be sure that what we are doing shall be effectual? Of course we do.

AFFIRMATIVE-PRAYER MEDITATION

(In this box are contained many requests for different kinds of healing, by a great many individuals. Every person who has put his name in there is in this room. Let me tell you *what* is going to happen, and *how* it is going to happen, so we will get right busy and begin to use what I am talking about. Because somebody by the name of John Smith put his name in here saying he would like to be healed of this, or wants this or that to happen, he has already identified his desire and need with our consciousness. And because we know that desire and need is met, we are already supplying the consciousness of that Power which can meet it, and we don't have to think about him. But together, this consciousness should rise to an attitude of thought where that demonstration or answer is inevitable and necessary; and I believe it will. But I want you to know that is the way it happens as we turn within to that divine Center which is both God and Man.)

Now at long last cleared from the stupidity of dogma, cleared from the skepticism of sophistry and the rebuttal of unbelief, cleared from all of the intolerance of overintellectualism and the spiritual stupidity of thinking that there is some God who favors one beyond the other: you and I join in the simplicity of our approach, the humbleness of our faith, the gentleness of our thought, the feeling of love from our own heart that at least would say to the poor and the weak and the suffering, "It doesn't have to be that way, perhaps. Perhaps there is a good greater than you have known. 'O thou beneath life's endless load, / Whose forms are bending low, / Who totter on the weary road / With troubled step and slow: / Ask now, for glad and golden hours / Come swiftly on the wing. / Oh, rest beside the weary road / And hear the angels sing.' "

Thou infinite and indwelling Presence, forever wonderful—God of heaven and earth, Maker of the rain and the mist, the sunshine and the shadow, back of the mountain, the valley, the summit, the fish in the ocean, and a thousand million waves spilling their crest of beauty on the moonlit beach across the trackless deep. Thou Beauty—Thou infinite Beauty flowing through the life of every person whose name is here. Divine Love and Compassion—our Love that will not let us go: we are entering, for ourselves and each one of these persons, into the name and power and spirit of that which is the essence of love and gladly surrenders all it has on the altar of its conviction. Lord God of Love, Father of givingness, Impulsion forever flowing full and free, that Love which cannot be repudiated: we love; and who shall deny the privilege of that affection?

There is a sense of love and givingness in the heart and mind and soul of each one of these names whom we embrace, embrace in the warmth of our own

heart, knowing their request is answered. Let wholeness come to each one. Let the eternality flow, the
enthusiasm of life. All the power and energy, all
the vitality that there is in the Universe shall flow
uninterrupted, torrent from the source of that river
which rises in eternal God. All the power that there
is, all the enthusiasm and energy and action that
there is in the Universe, *is* flowing through each person; and we know it.

All the peace, peace, peace—wonderful peace—
and all the sweetness—oh so sweet, so very sweet,
so beautiful—presses around them; wholeness, perfect circulation, perfect assimilation, perfect elimination. So shall Love come to them—Love, infinite and
deep and broad—and they shall embrace the Universe and be embraced by It. There shall be no sense
of isolation or loneliness. Happiness was made to
be happy. "There is ever a song somewhere, my
dear, and we shall sing it"; prosperity and success
beyond and above everything else—the final Good.
We are That which Thou art, eternal God, and we
know that Thou art that which we are forevermore.

And now may the peace and the joy of Life, the
song that sings, the morning star, the joy that claps
its hands in the leaves, the refreshing rain from
Heaven and the strength of the waves and the color
of the moonbeams and the sunset, the glory of the
rainbow of eternal promise and love and joy go with
you forever and forevermore.

CHAPTER 3

The Creative Power of Your Thoughts

I<small>T IS VERY</small> wonderful to be here again, and a wonderful thing to get this terrific audience here so early in the morning in hot weather.

This is the third in a subject which is designed to progressively arrive at certain definite conclusions. We are dealing with the creative power of Mind rather than with the creative power of our own thinking. Our own thinking utilizes a Mind principle which creatively acts upon it; therefore we tend to become like what we think.

There is a vast difference whether we say, "*I* create"—we all do create in a sense—or whether it is God, the Universe, a divine Principle, whichever you choose to call It, that creates. I do not make a rosebud—I plant a rosebush. I do not make a cucumber—I plant a seed, and something operates upon that seed. I do not create it. If I had to create even a cucumber, I would not know how to create it.

Now biology is the study of life in the human body, and all the biologies rolled into one have no more idea what life is than a jackrabbit has about mince pies; and I don't suppose a jackrabbit knows *anything* about a mince pie. All of the psychologists living, dealing with the operation of thought or emotions: there isn't one of them who knows what thought is, there isn't one of them who knows why feeling is, there isn't one of them who knows any more about what mind is than a child building little castles out of mud. It is interesting, isn't it?

Well, let's get the theologians' "dibs" in now. All the theologians in the world do not know any more about the nature of God than you and I. Remember, there are no prophets other than the wise. Every bible that was ever written was written by human beings, like we are. What I am trying to establish is that we don't know as much as we think we know. Someone has said, "I used to think I knew I knew, / But now I must confess: / The more I think I know I know, / I know I know the less."

Now science observes how these principles work. It studies the action and reaction of thought and emotion in the human mind; but it doesn't know what the human mind *is*. It studies the actions and reactions of life in the body; but it does not know what life *is*. Theology looks about it and speculates philosophically and idealistically on the nature of God. No doubt it is partly right; but "No man has seen God." And then they have the nerve to tell us which way we are going. This is amusing; it isn't even insulting. Such ideas can't insult anybody's intelligence, because there isn't anything there to insult it.

I must have an animosity to theology or I would never mention it. Isn't that strange! Shakespeare says, "Thou dost protest too much." It is a very interesting thing. Now physics is a study of universal energy acting everywhere. There isn't a physicist in the world who would even try to tell you what energy is. Let's take one other category, one that interests me particularly—that is, all of the creative arts. I love them above everything; they are so tied in to that which is beyond this mundane—for feeling, the creative imagination, revelation, and the inspiration. I look upon religion as one of the creative arts. Isn't that strange? Religion is the most creative thing in the world, and without it we are dead—temporarily.

No artist has ever seen beauty. He can't tell you what beauty looks like. He feels something and then he objectifies it. He paints a picture, or chisels something out of marble—an angelic figure—out of his imagination and feeling, but he never *saw* this; it is subjective. That is why we call what he does an "object" of art, meaning it is an objectification of the subjective mental state.

Here are the great realities of life, and no one has seen them. But we know a great deal about them by seeing what happens to people who hate instead of love; to people who cry instead of laugh; to people who have fear instead of faith: we are right in concluding that the nature of reality is affirmative.

If we discover that certain things that people put in the body are not good and when they don't put them in it is better, then we have a right to say, That is best. Therefore our sciences are built up pragmatically. That means *practically*, on observation—the gathering of a vast amount of data through endless experimentation, until at last modern science is able to say with complete certainty that all of these principles actually exist; but it also says with equal certainty that we must understand their laws to use them. And then their use becomes an individual thing.

Now this is the way it is with the creative power of

Mind. We do not have to be superstitious to believe that we are surrounded by creative Intelligence, which receives the impress of our thought and acts upon it, always tending to bring into our experience those things which are both conscious and subjective. Now let me explain that.

We have what we call our conscious thought; we hop and skip and jump along the surface of things, as we are doing now. But there is a deeper realm of mind. It is the same mind where all our habit patterns are stored, continuously repeating themselves until, as the Apostle said, "That which I do I would not, that which I would not I do. . . . O miserable man that I am, who shall deliver me from the body of this death?"*

Now that is psychologically sound, because Sigmund Freud said that a neurotic—that means an unhappy—thought pattern will repeat itself with monotonous regularity throughout life, just like it is playing a tune. And all psychology, psychiatry, and analytical work is based on the supposition that you can uncover these thoughts but that it is not the thoughts themselves that are creative. That is what you and I must learn.

Here is where we differ from psychology—not to repudiate it; we are not among those metaphysicians who deny everything they don't like. They have a peculiar coercion of their own. I believe everything is as real as it is supposed to be. If a person hurts, he hurts; if he feels badly, he cries. There is want, lack, and apparent limitation in human experience, and there is no use denying it. But perhaps it doesn't need to be; perhaps it is not

*Romans 7:19,24.

intended to be. It cannot be possible that life creates death. So when somebody asked Jesus what God's relationship to the dead is, he said, "He is not a God of the dead but of the living, for in His sight all are alive." That is wonderful. Just because you and I and the world have used this creative Power wrongly does not mean that *It* is wrong. Moses said, "The word is nigh unto thee, even in thine own mouth that thou shouldst know it and do it." He said that it is a blessing or a curse, according to the way we use it.

Now suppose that you and all people, while we have independent thinking and are individualizations of God or the Universe, each one a little different, are in reality all using the same Mind. There is only one Mind. Emerson said there is one Mind common to all individual men. The sixth chapter of Deuteronomy says, "Hear, O Israel: the eternal, the Lord Thy God, is one God." The Hindu says that everything that is is but a different kind of manifestation of the Only Thing that is; for He is one, undivided, indivisible, and ever present. And Einstein said that there is one law in nature, which is common to all laws. In other words, he said that there is one Law which dominates, governs, controls, synthesizes, unifies, coordinates every known law. Now this was his last pronouncement and has, to my knowledge, not been explained. *I* would understand it, anyway. But they are all saying what I am talking about.

There is only one Life. You and I do not have a mind separate from God. We have the Mind *of* God. The scripture says, "Let this mind be in you which was also in Christ Jesus." Now the word *Jesus* is a name, like John.

There are probably 50,000 boys in Mexico named Jesus. *Christ* has the same meaning as *the Buddha* or *the Atman** or *the Anointed* or *the Avatar* or *the Messiah* or *the Enlightened*. It means the spiritual Principle and the divine Presence. Let yourself be renewed by the renewing of your mind—that is, changing your thinking, putting off your "old man"—the habit—and putting on the new man: the exalted idea which is Christ.

Now we should get these simple things in mind, because they are fundamental to our whole system of thought; and I very much want you to take our course. If you have had it, review it. If you haven't had it, let nothing stop you from taking it. It is the most valuable course in metaphysics given in the world today, anywhere, by anyone—at any time; and it is to be given morning and evening—so you can take it; and the price is very low. *Just take the time.* It will do more for you than anything that ever happened to you. But this is the foundation of it: One Mind, and we use It.

Now I want to *prove* that to you. I don't want you to believe anything just because I say so—because I have a pretty good imagination and can think up a lot of things that are not so. But I am not a conscious liar; and everybody is an unconscious liar without meaning to lie.

I do not think we should make such a claim to divinity that we forget we are human. The human proclaims the divine; and here we are, a lot of little human beings doing the best we can—laughing and crying, singing and dancing, praying and exalting; then sometimes falling into

*In the sense "the innermost essence of each individual" (Webster's Collegiate Dictionary).

the depths of despair. Everyone does this, and the man who says he doesn't—he does. And so what? Let us accept it, nonresistantly; otherwise we shall be so inflexibly fighting life that we will get no fun out of it. You know, if the tree didn't bend a little before the wind, it would break off just like an icicle. Nature has provided a flexibility; and "He has tempered the wind to the shorn lamb." Nature is that way. Only man is inflexibile.

You watch people who have no flexibility; they have to say, "semantically speaking"—and that is stupid. We don't have to explain these things. If I say I love you, *that* is what I mean. We don't have to explain these simple things. We *feel* them. If I reach out and put my arms around you and hug you, you know this is an emotion of affection, and we don't have to say, "Is it like the affection of a cat? or a canary bird?" We *know*; because all language has come out of the *feeling* to action, and the impulsion and necessity of action. You know what *I* am talking about, and I know what *you* are talking about when you talk to me. Let's keep it simple.

And let's realize this: the profound thinkers of the universe didn't know very much more about it than you and I do; but they knew a lot of words we don't know the meaning of. Always remember this. I have made it a habit for 40 years when I am reading something that looks kind of tough to understand—and yet I know it is good—and I come to a sentence that I am not familiar with . . . I don't know just what it means—so I read it out loud three or four times and listen to it aloud; and then when I think I know what it means, I lay the book down and say it out loud to myself in my own language, three or four times. You will discover in reading you do not wish to transfer the written transcript into your vocabulary; that wouldn't be you. But you want *the thought*. The man has a thought, and you want it. Then you want to put it into your own words, because then you will never forget it. I have done that for 40 years, and it is a great aid. Just say, "Now I think the guy meant this: . . ."

Now we have to put the most abstract philosophy into our own simple words, or we are never going to get it. Then we shall know and understand and assimilate and digest and be able to use what the world knows. It is like our food: we eat it, we assimilate it; it goes into the blood and tissues and bone and the marrow and becomes the physical body.

So our thoughts—what we must learn—must go into another kind of a body, which becomes the body of our thinking; and you and I must know why we believe what we do without having to explain why it is true. And don't feel embarrassed about that. There isn't anyone in the world and all science and philosophy and religion—they are the only three sources through which knowledge comes . . . all of them combined cannot tell you how you can wiggle your finger. Now isn't that silly! They cannot tell you how the nuts and potatoes and soup and apple become hearts and livers and lungs and brain cells (if any). They can't tell you. They don't know, and they don't pretend to know. All they can know is that it happens. Therefore you have to keep the channels open, because where there is circulation, assimilation, and elimination, there is health in the body and normality in the mind; and now they are learning that the mind can't do that unless it has a strong spiritual emotion.

You might say, "Well, I came here to hear about the

creative power of thought"—and that is what I am talking about. If I came here to tell you how to make potatoes . . . now I can tell you how to *mash* them; if I came here to tell you how to do a painting or make lumber for building a house or create bricks—I couldn't tell you. We do not do these things. We can only be told how to put natural material together that becomes bricks. That is all we can be told. That is all anybody knows.

Now it is a funny thing: when it comes to speculative philosophy and religion, somebody rises up and says, "God has told me the whole works. Believe as I believe or go to the place that is hotter than L.A. has been recently" (but with no humidity). Wouldn't that be something? Now I treat hell and the devil very disrespectfully, because I haven't the slightest respect for either one, or for anybody's belief in either. It is all bunk. If anyone can tell me how we are going to learn to be happy by being unhappy, I want to hear about it. How are you going to keep dry by jumping in the water? It is beyond me.

The creative power of our thought—your ability to demonstrate, to give a treatment or say a prayer (I don't care what you call it) that will be effectual and produce a result—depends entirely on your knowing that you do not put anything in. You take it out. Never forget this. That is why Jesus said that the Kingdom of Heaven is like a child. "Suffer the little ones to come unto me and forbid them not, for of such is the Kingdom of Heaven." I love that. He was a man who spoke and thought as a child. Plato was no more profound, and far less simple.

Now you and I are scientific when we approach our principle just as a physicist or a biologist or a psychologist would approach his principle—impersonally saying, as Emerson said, "Naught unto me; tis Thou, God, who giveth; tis I who receive." Browning said (and Emerson said) that we are beneficiaries of the divine Fact. We are surrounded by a creative Intelligence which *does* operate upon our thought, whether we know it or not; it *does* create the body, making it sick or well; it *does* control our circumstances, making them happy or unhappy; it *can* bring any good into our lives that we can conceive rightly in cooperation with it—and it *will* and it *must*, and there won't be any question about it. Jesus said, "Heaven and earth shall pass away, but my word shall not, till all be fulfilled."

No one understands our science until he has come to see that, as the Apostle said, "I sowed, Apollos watered, but God gave the increase."* Every scientist in the world will say Amen to that. They will say, "We are using laws of Nature. Fortunately, we have discovered that they will work with invariable exactitude. We may rely upon them, because they are principles. We may learn new ways of using them. We may discover one day that what we call bondage is freedom." And I believe that. As Isaiah said, "He shall turn captivity captive."

I believe the power that makes us sick is the only power that can make us well. The power that impoverishes us is the only thing that can enrich us. If it were not so, the Universe would be a dualism and there would always be an evil contending against the Good; and God is One. "I am that I Am, beside which there is none other." I believe in absolute Unity. You and I are using the same Mind, the same Power. We wouldn't know each other if we weren't

*1 Corinthians 3:6.

using the same Mind. But we are individuals in It, and all of It is back of each one of us. Just as you and I do not create the watermelon but may so comply with Nature that one little seed will produce half a dozen watermelons, each with a thousand seeds in it—there is a principle of multiplicity—so you and I by conscious cooperation with the laws of Mind reacting to our thinking can and will and must and do bring good or ill into our lives.

Now keep it as simple as that—because if you are so fortunate as to decide to take our course, you are going to learn how to be a practitioner. It is the greatest good that can come into anybody's life. You are not going to be taught any superstition or dogma; and you are not going to be taught that only the Religious Scientists can jump into the water and not get wet.

One provision I have made is that whenever I shuck off this mortal coil, there isn't a thing of mine that whoever is left here can't take out and put in the ashcan the next day. Isn't that wonderful? I would not wish to perpetuate my stupidity, my ignorance, and my limitation. Someone will come along and do it better. "Ever as the spiral grew / He left the old house for the new." "Build thee more stately mansions, O my soul, / While the swift seasons roll. / Leave thy low-vaulted past; / Let each new temple, nobler than the last, / Shut thee from Heaven with a dome more vast, / Till thou at last art free, / Leaving thy outgrown shell / By life's unceasing sea."

The last word will never be spoken; *you* are the last word. *You* are the revelator. *You* are the medium and the mediator between yourself—which is John and Mary, the human Christ, the Incarnation—and God the absolute. No one shall lay a gift of God upon your altar to the glory of the Eternal but yourself, for *you* are the gift. Lowell said, "Bubbles we earn with a whole soul's casting, / Tis Heaven alone that is given away; / Tis only God may be had for the asking." "Ask no man." Ask not of me or Bill or Reg* or George; we are those struggling toward the Light. "For what was I, / An infant crying in the night, / An infant crying for the light, / And with no language but a cry."

But "the feeble hands and helpless, / Groping blindly in the darkness, / Touched God's right hand in that darkness / And are lifted up and strengthened." Be simple. You alone shall meet Him face to face in the Secret Place of the Most High, the tabernacle of the Almighty in your own soul, where God lives. This is the starting point of all creativity. *Now* your thought will be operated upon.

What is more logical than to go about it definitely, and for every negation create an affirmation—? Instead of saying, "I cannot," say, "I can; you can; he can; we can; they can; it can—God can." There is a Power that *will*— in simplicity. Then, when the other thoughts come up, deny them. It will erase them gradually. It takes time. Be patient. You are working with an absolute certainty, and you see that you don't feel obligation or responsibility.

You and I don't know how to make a liver. We know how to use thought that will heal a liver that looks bad. We do not know how to make a brain. We can use thought that will so stimulate the brain cells we have that they shall multiply along the line of our desire. We do not know how to create Substance. We can use thought as realization and receptivity to Substance until everywhere

*See p. 5. *Reg* refers to Reginald Armor, the earliest of Dr. Holmes' associates besides his brother Fenwicke.

we turn, the supply we need for our daily things will come to us.

Couldn't we see abundance everywhere? How many leaves on the trees, how many stars—how vast is everything! And all this vastness belongs to us. It is all pouring itself through us. How much are we receiving definitely, deliberately, consciously, day by day, everywhere we look? Couldn't we see happiness, even where it looks sad—?

"Oh dry those tears, life was not made for sorrow." "There is ever a song somewhere, my dear; there's ever a song—somewhere." And love: couldn't we learn to love everybody? And someday when our arms are encircling God and the Universe and humanity, we shall know that God is Love. No one will have to tell us. No one will ever have to prove it to us. And all the abstractions and speculations of the human mind shall fall like dust; and the Light that is direct and simple shall reveal to you and to me.

There is a Power greater than we are that we use. It is so very simple; and as you study this course—and I say you would be very foolish not to—remember, one with God is a majority. We may *know* the Truth; we can only *believe* what is not so. If all the people in the world believed what is not so, and only one person knew the Truth, that one person who knew the Truth would repudiate the belief of all the rest of them. That is why Jesus said, "The words that I speak unto you, they are Spirit and they are Life."

Just as surely as tomorrow shall come and the sun again shall rise across the darkness of the horizon and spill its beauty and warmth to awaken the valleyland into fertility, human beings into warmth and color—so you and I, looking across the new horizon of a greater possibility, may walk forth and meet the living God and feel His embrace and know His Presence and may come to know at last of the infallibility of a Power that the simplest may use, as a child is held in place by gravitational force. "O living truth that shall endure / When all that seems shall suffer shock, / Rise on the rock and make us pure." May the living presence of the eternal God awaken within each one of us now the realization of peace and joy.

O Infinite Beauty, diffused and infused, spilling Itself over us and flowing through us in the majestic harmony of warmth and color and feeling: our minds are open to Thy divine influx. O infinite Sweetness beyond compare, O sweet Presence: flow through us in Joy. To You we surrender all littleness and all fear and all doubt, that the living fountain from the eternal River of Life flowing from the Mind of God shall renew our vigor, remake our strength, ennoble our being, heal our bodies and fortunes, and bring peace to the waiting heart. Thou Love that evermore embraces us: we surrender all hurt to Thee. In Thy Wisdom make us wise; in Thy Light give us light; and in Thy Joy shall we laugh as children playing on the shores of time as the great ocean of eternity evermore flows and flows into our being. Amen.

AFFIRMATIVE-PRAYER MEDITATION

(A great many names have been placed in this box. Some have requested healing, some perhaps love and friendship, betterment of circumstances. Now each one knows what he has asked for. Our treatment and our consciousness united, I believe, will act for each one—if he receives, without question, the good he has asked for. Don't try to see how it can be brought about; just say, "I am accepting the fulfillment of this." And remember: when you treat someone, you identify your prayer or treatment with him. It is for him. Then your whole time is spent realizing within yourself something about him—always on the supposition that I have talked about this morning: that Something acts upon your thought toward your identification. That is, I am treating: "This word is for John Smith. He lives at such-and-such a place." You forget about him. Then you form your statements to cover the need, sometimes denying what appears and affirming its opposite—it doesn't matter—until you yourself are convinced. Now Something greater than you are operates upon it. It is a law in nature. *It is a law.*)

As we turn within to that divine Presence which is both God and Man, unifying us all together in Love, the first thing we do is *realize* that Love and turn to each other and mentally embrace each other. I love you. I adore you. I surrender that part of myself which is pure Spirit to you in love. It is wonderful. And you do to me. And we are embracing each other in love—oh so sweet, so very tender, so intimate love. So shall joy come to us.

There is one infinite Peace now indwelling us and each person particularly who has put his name in this box. Now we are going to bless him. God bless him or her. Let him receive the blessing; it is real. We bless him—and everything within him is blessed, and everything that doesn't belong to him is eliminated; and everything that belongs to Perfection is manifest.

There is one Life, that Life is God, that Life is his life. It is perfect *now*, and It is manifesting in him now, right now. Let him receive it. Not from you and me, but from out of this thought, from out of this great Mind which is God, this Power which is good, this Law which is perfect. It is so, and this word shall continue and it shall prosper. Everything that this person does shall prosper. The way is made perfect and plain and straight and immediate and permanent and happy and whole and prosperous before him. All the love there is and all the friendship that there is is delivered to him. There is no resentment; he has surrendered every hate, every resentment, every doubt, and embraces the universe of wholeness. So shall Love guide him and govern him and Peace flow through him, the Light of Heaven go with him. Sweet friend in God, you are blessed and all your ways prospered. That which does not belong has fallen away, and the limbs are strengthened and the circulation is perfect. Every organ and action and function of the body proclaims the divinity, the harmony, the unity, and the perfection of Good; and you are prospered in Love now and forevermore. Amen.

And now as we go into the great joy of life, the light of the living Spirit shall go before us, the love of the eternal God shall wrap us around, and we shall be embraced and we shall embrace. So may it be that there shall go forth from us the Light of Heaven. May every person we meet be blessed and may every situation we contact be prospered. We surrender ourselves to this—we dedicate ourselves to this—in love, in joy, and in gladness. May the eternal Spirit go with us, guiding and guarding us forevermore. Amen.

CHAPTER 4

How to Enjoy Abundant Health
for Creative Living I

In October 1957 Dr. Holmes was looking forward to sharing an evening lecture with David Fink, M.D. He was as well renowned a medical personality as a devoted metaphysician with a strong belief in the teachings of Dr. Holmes. They had selected a topic for the October 29th talks to a joint session of classes at the Institute of Religious Science at 6th and New Hampshire, Los Angeles. The topic for the evening was based on the idea that your attitude could make you sick or make you well.

Dr. Fink elected to speak during the first half of the evening and Dr. Holmes the closing half. They decided to label the entire evening "How to Enjoy Abundant Health for Creative Living." Dr. Holmes was particularly impressed with what Dr. Fink had to say about sacrifice. In fact he thought of it as "sacrifice without morbidity." He stressed that no psychiatrist or metaphysician would ever make anybody more whole than the psychiatrist or metaphysician himself was. The talk that follows was Dr. Fink's contribution. Chapter 5 is Dr. Holmes'.

DAVID FINK, M.D.

I CAN'T TELL YOU how happy it makes me to be here with you. How many of you have heard me before?

Oh, gracious, I'm with friends, then—I hope!

Of course, it puts me under some obligation to say something that you haven't heard before. I imagine you would be pretty tired of hearing me say the same old things. So I won't—except to say, by way of parenthesis: always practice relaxing your muscles, and you will feel better. Relax them at every possible opportunity; never use muscles in tension that you don't have to use.

A certain woman who was a very dear friend of mine —I loved her; she went on to a better world to my great sorrow—used to say to me, "Doctor Fink, you aren't telling me anything new. When I work, I work hard; when I sit down, I relax; and when I worry, I go to sleep." She didn't worry, and her life was an inspiration to me and to my wife. She was a wonderful woman, a wonderful mother, a wonderful friend.

Well, that is the way it goes. You can't keep them with us always, and all we can do is emulate and try to live up to the best that our friends demonstrate and expect of us.

Now I happen to be, as you know, a physician and metaphysician; and the two are not incompatible by any means. When I first came here last Saturday night, I was registering at a motel and a call came in at the desk. A young man was sick with influenza; so they wanted a doctor, and they couldn't get one on Saturday night. They asked me if I would go and see the boy—an engineer just coming in from South Dakota to work at Douglas. He had a temperature of 103 and was the kind of person who could have had very serious results from his troubles.

I felt that the surest way to get him well quick was to treat his mind. You know, I can't treat the virus—nobody can—but I could treat his mind. And he made such a remarkable recovery that anyone who was willing to open his eyes and his mind and his heart could not have failed to be impressed by the rate of recovery. And it wasn't his great constitution that got him well, but a constitution that was adopted all before he ever came on this earth.

He was helped by God; and because he was willing to believe and have faith, he got well quickly. It is so simple. You know there is, of course, a "natural" explanation for everything—a physical explanation for everything. The physical explanation is that disease processes are augmented by an adrenalurgic* reaction. It has been demonstrated in the laboratory by Hans Selye, who made experiments on poor harmless rats that weren't doing him any harm—and he found out, by these animal experiments, what Ernest Holmes has been saying all these years.

At any rate, the disease reactions—the response to disease—can be augmented or decreased by attitudes, such as when this man was receptive to a religious attitude, when he was willing to believe that God would get him well, if only he didn't *try* to get well. *"Don't try to get well,"* I said; "don't worry about your troubles. You can't *help* but get well if you only let God cure you

*This should perhaps be *adrenergic*.

and relax. Take it easy; and remember: it is only a matter of a few hours and you will be healed." The adrenalurgic reaction ceased, and his temperature fell naturally. It is so simple. People make themselves sick with their attitudes.

Now what I am going to talk to you about tonight is how to enjoy abundant health for creative living. Abundant health, of course, is worthless in itself—completely worthless. A patient of mine, a diabetic who suffered from diabetes ever since she was 14, had made a "career" of curing herself of diabetes, and of course all she had done was make herself worse and worse. So I asked her: "What would you do if you were well? What do you want to *accomplish*?" And she told me that what she wanted to do was work in the Church of Religious Science and conduct group therapy, have discussion groups in her home, talking about metaphysics and how to improve her own understanding of life.

"Well," I said, "what is stopping you? Go ahead and do it, and let the diabetes take care of itself; take it as a matter of course. If it helps you to take insulin once a day, regard that as a minor annoyance and take it and forget it and get busy with your metaphysics and the group you are gathering, and work with Doctor Whitehead* up in Monterey. *Let's get something done.*" And she did; and her blood sugar fell. It is as simple as that.

Now what I am talking about is this: you can have abundant health if you don't search for it, if you don't seek it. Don't make abundant health your goal in life,

*Carleton Whitehead, Religious Science minister.

because it will be a very elusive goal. It is like seeking happiness: you don't find happiness by seeking it; you find happiness by doing something which makes your life meaningful. Then happiness comes to you like sunshine. It comes to you from without. It just pours in on you. You *are* happiness—but you mustn't seek it, any more than you must seek health. You must seek *creative living* —and you can have abundant health for creative living, if you make creative living your goal. *That* is what I want to talk about.

How can you achieve success? Why is it that some people are just naturally lucky and other people aren't? How can you be one of those lucky ones? You *can* be—you can *all* be lucky; because "good luck" is the fruit of your character. The kind of character that you develop, that you make for yourself, that you create will make your own good luck, your own abundant health for creative living.

Just what would you like to accomplish? Let's be very practical about this. This is one of the things I ask my patients: *What do you want?* One patient says, "I would like to lose weight; but every time I diet, I gain." Another patient says, "I would like financial security; but every time I try to make money or invest it, I lose money." And another person says, "I would like to have friends and be popular; but people just don't like me. I am always lonely. I just don't have any friends. There is something about me that chases people away from me, people I would have as friends." Another person says, "I feel gloomy, I feel sad, I feel blue. I want to get rid of my depressions."

Okay; these are just *some* things. Others say, "I would like to enjoy greater self-confidence." Others say, "I would like to make my marriage work; but my husband doesn't like me, and he doesn't treat me right, and I think he wants to get rid of me." Or it might be a husband who says that about his wife—he wants to make his marriage work. Another man says, "I am an alcoholic and would like to lick the alcohol habit and achieve sobriety." And of course I always say, *"Why?"* And if he would say, *"Because I want to accomplish something worthwhile,"* I would say, "You have already achieved your sobriety, my friend. Just keep your mind on wanting to accomplish something worthwhile and you will never in this wide world ever again take another alcoholic drink."

These are the things people would like to accomplish —these among the 101 other things which they think would make them happy. Each one of us has his own ideas of what would make him happy, what he would like to accomplish, what would amount in his life to creative living. And I say, *any* of these things, *all* of these things, are within your power to take. They are yours for the asking. All you have to do is to go about these projects intelligently and you can't fail.

That is what I am talking about tonight: how you can go about these projects intelligently. What makes you fail. What makes you succeed. The answer is so absurdly simple that I am sometimes ashamed to get up before an intelligent group and tell them, because it seems to me that anything so simple must surely have occurred to all of you. But I am the kind of person who has to say the obvious anyway; so if I bore you, it won't be too long.

So I am going to tell you what I think makes some people fail in achieving the happiness they seek, in achieving the success they look for—what makes them fail in achieving creative living and makes them deprive themselves of abundant health: *what makes them fail.* In one word, it is their *attitudes. Attitudes* make you fail or succeed—your *attitudes.*

Now what is an attitude? An attitude is the way you are prepared to act in any situation. The way you are prepared to act in a situation is your attitude. You may not know how you are prepared to act in this situation or that situation; but you always *are* prepared to act. And it is *knowing how* you are prepared to act that enables you to fulfill your attitudes. Now I think that is worth a little more elaboration, discussion, and clarification.

The situations in our lives are a part of a flow of life. Situations in which we live flow around us, past us, constantly. The situations are constantly changing, in states of flux, in states of constant motion. As each situation arises, we are prepared to react to that situation in one way or another. The situation within us—our interior environment—is constantly changing. Either you have eaten and are full right up to here; or else you haven't eaten, and your backbone is pressing against your stomach, you are so empty. Your interior situation is constantly changing, and your exterior situation is constantly changing, and how you are prepared to act in one situation or another will determine your happiness or your unhappiness, your success or your failure, your abundant health or your abundant lack of health.

Now *attitudes*: I think I might as well explain this a little more fully.

Let's say you are going into a department store and you expect to be waited upon. Now of course this won't happen in the great city of L.A., where all of the department stores are loaded with so many good things, and the help is so well trained, etc., etc. But if you were to go into a smaller community where the help is not so well trained, you would find that what you expect and what you get are two very different things.

If you go into the store expecting the clerk to have at his disposal an unlimited quantity of goods; if you go into that same store and expect the clerk to know the stock perfectly; if you go there expecting him to have an intuitive sense of your needs and what you can afford and what you want to buy; if you go there expecting the prices to be well within your reach for exactly what you hope to find (even if you don't know exactly what you are looking for when you go into the store)—and you meet a clerk who is indifferent; if you meet a clerk who doesn't know the stock; and if the stock itself is limited in its quantity: then you are going to be frustrated.

Your attitude is one thing, the situation is another, and frustration results. And as a result of frustration, a whole chain of events occurs within your body, including muscle tension; including your intestines going into spasms; including your glands of internal secretion pouring forth adrenalin into your system; including your rapid breathing and dry mouth; and so on and so forth. And this will give rise to a feeling of anger, or hostility.

But if you were to go into that store with a *different* attitude, saying, "I'll just go and see what happens; I'll treat whatever happens as a matter of course. I'm not under any particular obligation to buy. I'll look around and do my best, and my attitude will be one of hopeful expectancy; but it won't be one of being positive I am going to get exactly what I want when I want it, or even better than I had hoped."* If that is your attitude, then you won't be frustrated; and furthermore, you won't be suffering from all the processes which lead to harmful emotions and disagreeable dealings. You can't change the clerk's attitudes.

Let's talk about the woman, for instance, who wanted to lose weight. What is her food attitude? Her food attitude is one of weak self-indulgence. Her food attitude is that food represents to her the love she did not receive when she was a child. And so whenever she is bored or whenever she is disappointed or whenever any disagreeable sensation or feeling or situation arises in her life, she runs to the icebox and makes herself a sandwich. And that is why it is impossible for her to lose weight with that food attitude. The food attitude is all wrong.

Another person who wants to get rid of that depression has a self-attitude that is punitive—self-punishing. That person is depressed. Why? Because he or she (and I have both he's and she's in my practice) feels guilty for things that have been done in the past. And because she is constantly feeling guilty, she feels that she is going to be punished. She is afraid of being punished. She is afraid of hellfire; and her fear of hellfire is so great that she

*This is not quite Ernest Holmes' teaching. See, for example, *The Science of Mind*, where he says, in a slightly different context, "We need only turn over to Intelligence our highest conceptions . . . and there will be delivered to us something much finer than it was possible to picture" (p. 645).

furnishes the oil for the flame. It is that attitude, that self-attitude, punitive self-attitude—that attitude that Judas had that makes her suffer in a minor way what Judas suffered in a major way; and I think that most suicides like those of Judas arise from feelings of guilt and feelings of despair.

Now a normal attitude, a healthy attitude, a simple attitude that every physician and metaphysician would have her take would be that of trust in the infinite love of God. You know, no one could be worse than a traitor. I think a traitor is about the lowest form of life. A man whom you depend on who goes over to the enemy is pretty low; and any man who has been a traitor has the right, he might think, to feel guilty. And one of the greatest traitors in history was Saint Peter, who lived with the Lord, who saw his miracles, who had opportunities such as none of you will ever have of being in contact—physical contact—with Jesus. And yet three times he denied his Lord. Three times in a row.

What a traitor! And yet what happened? He had one saving grace: he did not lose hope; he did not despair; he did not go into a depression and say, "Oh what a worthless worm am I!" Instead, he trusted in the infinite love of God and became the first and greatest saint—the founder of the Church, or at least the first leader of the Church of Jesus.

Now if the Lord can forgive St. Peter, who was a traitor, and take him and make him the keeper of the Keys of Heaven, why should any of us who have never had those opportunities worry about the mistakes or the sins or the evil that we have done in the past? All we have to do is be sorry and resolve not to repeat our mistakes. And as soon as a person takes that point of view—I don't care whether you call it the advice of a physician who says, "Forget it," or the advice of a metaphysician who says, "Believe in God, and God will heal you"—he is free from his depression, because he has changed his own self-attitude. He has ceased to punish himself. He has ceased to put himself in the role of the devil, roasting himself in hell, and he has put himself in the position of the angels who are lifting him up to Heaven.

Your attitudes can make you well or your attitudes can make you sick—your self-attitudes and your attitudes toward other people. The person who says, "My husband doesn't love me": we went into her case and what did we find? Her husband is the kind of person who wants a mother. He wants a *motherly* wife—the kind of a woman who will make her husband's career, her husband's happiness, and her husband's success *her* career. That is the career in life she must adopt if she is going to make her husband happy, or at least satisfied, because that is his need.

And what about her? She is a very good daughter, she is very good to her mother; and being a good daughter is more important to her than being a good wife. And then she says, "I want to make my marriage work; I want my marriage to succeed." Well, it can't succeed with that attitude, any more than the person can lose weight whose food attitude is that food is a substitute for human friendship and affection. Food is *not* a substitute. And as soon as she changes her attitude toward her husband from that of being a critical sister to that of being a devoted wife, her marriage cannot fail.

If you want to make anything succeed, you have first of all to analyze the attitudes which have given rise to the failure. If you want to get rid of your depression, I assure you: get rid of your feelings of guilt and fear of punishment and you will never feel depressed. You *can't* feel depressed. You will wake up singing. But you will never wake up singing if you keep harping on the past.

I remember one woman who badgered the life out of a priest because she ate pie on Friday and she said, "Maybe there was lard in the pie crust";* and the priest said, "Go say ten Hail Marys and God will forgive you"—which was very foolish advice on the part of the priest, I think, because it only made the woman sure she *had* committed a sin. So she said ten Hail Marys; and then she wan't sure God had forgiven her. So she came back to the priest the next afternoon and told him the same story and the same story and the same story, until finally he said, "Go to a psychiatrist"—which was perhaps one way of saying, "Go to the devil!"

So she came to see me, naturally, and I had to give her a religious instruction—tell her that if she had eaten not *lard in pie,* but if she had eaten *the whole hog* on Friday, it would make no difference. The important thing is how did she feel about the future? How did she feel about God? Does she believe in God or doesn't she? If she believes in God, God isn't going to worry about her nibbling away at a little piece of pig. The pig was already dead. Of course, if she had bitten a live pig, it might have been different. That would have been *really* cruel!

*Refers to the obligatory abstention by Catholics (at that time) from eating meat on Friday.

Now all of your attitudes cluster into what they call *character traits*. You make your own "luck" with your character traits. A character trait is a cluster of attitudes that determines how you are going to behave in a more or less organized situation. Some people have the character trait of always exploiting their friends. Other people have the character trait of picking the "cards" of their past days—each card a different episode—shuffling them up, and dealing them out to their husbands at two o'clock in the morning, in different combinations. A kind of devilish solitare I would call it.

There are a number of character traits; the character trait of a man who is trying to get something for nothing, who doesn't realize that God created this world on the theory that if you don't work, you don't eat—and he thinks he can beat the game. And naturally he is always losing money on the horse races, and wondering why his savings are all frittered away. *Naturally*; because the character traits, which represent a whole cluster of attitudes—dependency, and desire to exploit someone, get something for nothing, etc.—the character traits which are his techniques for living (that is what a character trait is: a technique for living) are character traits that are bound to get him into trouble.

Now my thesis—I am still talking about abundant health for creative living—is that anyone who does not have abundant health for creative living should examine his character traits—his techniques for dealing with situations. Each character trait represents a cluster of attitudes—what he expects of himself, or what he expects of life. If he wants abundant health for creative living, let him examine his character traits.

Now as I said at Asilomar, one sure way—one simple way—of acquiring the right character traits is to *stop, look,* and *listen.* Look at the people in real life or in fiction or in biography or in autobiography who have the character trait that you would have, that you admire. Hero worship is the beginning of growth. No one can grow into a man who does not have an idea of a man's role in this world, and little boys usually acquire this notion of what it is to be a man. They acquire it from observing their fathers and other men in their immediate environment when they get to be about six or eight years old; and they become, in a way, hero-worshipers and grow up—actually grow up into manhood—not by accident but by copying the behavior of people whom they consider manly. And the same thing applies to women. The best thing that can happen to a girl is to have a mother whom she can admire, emulate, and finally leave. It is a good thing for a girl to know how to untie apron strings. The time to tie an apron string is when you go into the kitchen and not when you go into your mother's home.

It is through hero-worship, through analyzing and admiring the character traits of those whom you would emulate that you acquire the character traits which enable you to grow into abundant health and creative living.

Now there are five steps to abundant health in creative living, and I am going to give them to you. First of all, there is *the goal.* The goal represents your visualization of the situation that will satisfy your needs. You have to visualize the goal first, whatever it may be—a happy marriage, a wealth of friends, a more spiritual life— thousands of goals, each one of which represents your needs; and of course every rounded person has more than one goal. You might want good taste in interior decorating. Whatever your goal is, you visualize that. That is number one.

Number two: you have to visualize yourself as the kind of person who has the character traits that make for the kind of success that you want. We will call that *vision*. Seeing yourself, thinking of yourself, as a different kind of person—as the kind of person whom you aspire to be.

Goal first. Vision second.

Number three: *repetition*. Constantly keep in mind the goal and the vision—the goal you are trying to achieve, and the vision of yourself as the kind of person who is fit to achieve that goal.

The fourth you might not like. The fourth step is *sacrifice*. My friends, there is nothing in this world in the way of abundant health for creative living that can be achieved without sacrifice. Sacrifice is as real, as fundamental, as religious, as medical, as scientific, as this table and as God Himself. One of the earliest stories of the primitive Hebrews began with the thought of sacrifice. I think it was Abraham who was asked to sacrifice his own son to God and showed his willingness to give up the thing he loved the most. And then God gave him a substitute to sacrifice in its place.

There is nothing in religion that means a thing that does not involve sacrifice. I have often heard these social workers say, "Give till it hurts." I wouldn't take anything from a man who gave till it hurt. I would be too proud. I say, "Give until it feels good." Give until it feels good. If you do not lose your whole self in something, you will never gain anything. It is only the person who dedicates himself to something more worthwhile than himself who achieves his own self. The essence of success is sacrifice, if you want abundant health for creative living.

Health is like one of those plans they had during the Depression: $30 every Thursday, or something like that. The idea was that every Thursday, everybody was to be given $30 in scrip, and it was to be dated; and if it wasn't spent within one week, the money was no good. Well, your health is that way too: if you don't spend it, you can't buy anything with it; it is "dated." So the essence of creative living is sacrifice. You have to give up a hundred things to achieve one thing.

You know, the compass is a circle, and they divided it into 360 because they used to think the year had 360 days. So every compass point points to one degree in 360. And if you go in any single direction, following your compass, you are giving up the opportunity of going in 359 different directions. You have to make up your mind to give up what you don't want and really don't care about in order to get what you *do* want and you *do* care about.

And that goes for the woman who wants to lose weight; for the man who wants greater economic security; for the person who wants friends and to be popular; for the person who wants to feel free from fear; right to the person who wants to get rid of this depression: she has to give up a *pleasure*. The woman who wants to be free from depression has to give up the pleasure of feeling guilty. She has to quit enjoying punishing someone, including—and particularly—herself directly, and everyone around her indirectly; for she spreads unhappiness the way she might spread a bad odor. But if she would love herself, feel that she has God within herself, and if she would give up this notion that she is adequate to judge herself, that she knows more about God than God does: if she would give up that pride, she would give up her depression and she would be happy.

And now the fifth thing. In order to change your character traits in the direction of better health for more creative living, you have to have a *goal*; you have to see yourself as the person who is fit to achieve that goal; you have to constantly keep it in mind by continuous *repetition*, such as you find in the magazine *Science of Mind*—repetition, daily repetition; *sacrifice*, give up, that which doesn't count for that which does. And then finally, number five—is *faith*. Faith. *Expect results*.

(And incidentally, in the form of repetition I forgot to mention that I include prayer. Prayer and repetition are practically synonymous. Constantly feel the presence of God through prayer.)

Faith is the last step. *You expect results*. Good results come to the man who expects them. No one ever catches the train who thinks he is going to miss the train and feels, "Well, there is no use going to the station; I will miss it anyway." That man will never, never, *never* board the train.

But the man who says, "Why sure; I have an hour. It only takes 45 minutes to get there. Let's go!"—that man will be on the train when the conductor gives the engineer the highball. *Expect results*. Now others have done it. As I say, you are all intelligent people, and perhaps you knew all this before I started to talk. I don't know. But it seems so simple, it seems so direct, it seems so obvious that it embarrassed me, in a way, to get up here like a little boy reciting the multiplication table before a group of mathematicians. If others have done it, *you* can do it; your friends can do it.

So perhaps if you do know all these things, you will forgive me. I have organized them, perhaps, for you— have told you how to achieve abundant health for creative living and organized it for you; and perhaps you can pass the good word on to your friends and show them how they too can enjoy abundant health for creative living, by changing their character traits to achieve the things they want to achieve. And they can do it by having a definite *goal*; by *seeing* themselves as the kind of person who deserves to achieve that goal; by *repeating* the goal constantly (and by prayer, prayer, prayer); by *sacrifice* of everything that is not essential to the achievement of that goal; and by having *faith* in results.

Now Ernest Holmes said he was going to talk right away, and so I am going to give you time to get some air and relax, and you will be more receptive to what my dear friend Ernest Holmes has to tell you.

CHAPTER 5

How to Enjoy Abundant Health for Creative Living II

T HE MOST DIFFICULT thing in the world is to talk the way Doctor Fink has just talked to us—simplicity. I have often thought of it in reading the words of Jesus and of Plato, who taught pretty much the same thing. But Plato is so profound, you don't know what he is talking about; and Jesus is so simple, no one realized that his simplicity exposed his profundity—because they both taught only two or three very simple facts.

The first of these is that we are living in a spiritual Universe now, in which an infinite Intelligence eternally lives, equally distributed throughout time and space, impersonal to everyone until It is personalized in and through that person; and that of a necessity there are prototypes, archetypes, or ideas, or spiritual patterns in the invisible for everything that is in the visible; and that naturally we are tied into this pattern.

But when the things that David told us about happen, we don't untie the pattern, but we untie *ourselves* from it to a certain degree, and that whether it is by prayer, medication, or surgery or psychiatry or spiritual mind

treatment. All in the world we do is what Emerson referred to when he said to get your bloated nothingness
out of the way of the divine circuit to restore that which
in itself needs no restoration; God isn't sick or poor or
miserable or unhappy. And I was particularly delighted
at his idea of sacrifice without morbidity—not sacrifice
from the standpoint of sin and salvation, the fall and
the redemption. It is like washing a window so you can
see through it.

It is like getting rid of what *doesn't* belong in order that
what *does* belong shall be evident; or "loosing" that "imprisoned splendor." It is letting go and letting God, really.
And I thought also of something I discovered when I was
a kid, about ten years old. We were brought up without
any fear; we were not taught there is a hell or a devil or
any of this damned nonsense (that is all it is). Someone
says, "You shouldn't speak that way about it." I *like* to
speak that way about it; that keeps me from being frustrated too. But the harm that a wrong perspective of God
has done would make countless angels weep. Therefore
I always say, "I thank the God that is, that the God that
is believed in, *isn't*." If He were, it would be terrible.

But I discovered then, in a retired minister (I didn't
know what he was until 30 years after that), that he had
no condemnation for anything or anyone. And I used to
wonder about it. I used to take his hand and walk down
through the countryside, and I always felt close to Something that was different from anything else that I had ever
contacted. It is very vivid in my memory now. It was at
least 30 years ago and maybe 40, because I am approaching the age of what they call the "Ancient of Days."

I know now what David told us—I have known for

years—that in the Universe in which we live (this is my way of saying it) we did not create ourselves, we didn't put the mountains up there, we didn't put each other here. This is what happened to Job. He told God he had done everything that a good guy should do, and he told God over and over again what a good guy he was. And finally God said, "Well, you are a very wonderful man, Job; but where were you when I planted the North Star and sent the wind blowing? I just don't remember seeing you around." This is when Job fell flat on his face, for at last this got him. He had gotten in the way of "the divine circuit." His self-righteousness was a condemnation; because we don't have to be either condemned *or* righteous.

As Emerson said, when virtue is self-conscious, it is vicious. Just try to spend a whole day with someone who knows he is good; and if you have never thought of murder before, you will contemplate it before night. There is nothing you can do with them—and murder is against the law.

This Universe in which we live we did not make, nor did we create ourselves; but we seem to have the privilege of a freedom, Tolstoy said in *War and Peace*—we have "freedom within the laws of inevitabilities." In other words, our freedom cannot infringe the nature of the Universe. When everybody believed the world was flat, the only thing that was flattened was their experience—because the world was round. But they did, and we all do, project into the universe of Reality the illusion or delusion or false conclusion or confusion of our own minds and look at it and sometimes worship it as God, sometimes fear it as destiny, sometimes shudder as though it were the imposition of some cosmic energy or force which is malevolent—because we worship our evil more than we do our good.

Somebody said to me one day, relative to a certain evangelist whose name is unknown, but a very good man who located Hell under Manhattan Island (and I was so glad is wasn't Hollywood, because I had so often said it *was*)—he said to me, "Don't you believe in Hell?" and I said, "No." And he said, "Well, this man describes it"; and I said, "He has traveled a great deal more than I have; it is probably perfectly all right: he has just been places and seen things." Which made me think of the little bus-boy who was attending a banquet given by the Travelers Club, and this man who had been a world traveler was speaking, saying how he had fished in the seven seas and shot polar bear in the arctic and hunted out on the veldt and done this and that—and everyone naturally was enthusaistic and quite overcome by his greatness, where he had been and what he had seen. And this little busboy pulls his coat and says, "Mister, did you ever have the D.T.'s?" and he said, "Certainly not!" And the kid said, "You ain't been nowhere and you ain't seen nothin'!" So it is all relative.

Here is the Universe in which we live, which we did not create; but by some Power that shapes our ends, "rough hew them though we may," we have this freedom within the laws of inevitabilities. As David has said, we can make ourselves unhappy, impoverished, and everything else—because this is our freedom. And therefore our freedom makes our bondage possible. And if it were not possible to have the bondage, we would be automatons and could not have the freedom. It is one of those abstractions that we must not lose sight of, because if we could keep that in mind until we see through it, we should understand the nonviolence of Gandhi and the nonresistance of Jesus in a fluidic Universe which Emerson said we see as a solid fact but God views as liquid law.

And so we have that freedom—not to change the Universe, and not really to change the intrinsic nature of each other, nor really to change the intrinsic nature of *ourselves*; but to go with the tide of cosmic affairs or resist it—and in doing it, project our reaction in a universe of Reality until to us it becomes, as some of the ancients called it, Maya, the world of illusion. It isn't exactly illusion; it is *delusion*. It is not a thing in itself. And I discovered after all these years what this retired preacher knew and I felt. He no longer condemned himself; and because he didn't, it was impossible for him to project his condemnation on the Universe or on others. And there is no other condemnation.

Now there are two incidents in the Bible . . . of course, I don't believe the Bible literally. I don't think there ever was an Adam and an Eve. There was a Moses; but I don't think there was a Garden of Eden or a serpent that talked, or anything like that. This is a symbolism. And God came "walking in the garden in the cool of the day" to talk with Adam and Eve; and Adam looked down and saw he didn't have on any pants, so he jumped behind a cactus, and God said, "Adam, where art thou?" and Adam said, "I have hid, God." And God said; "This is funny; we have always been friends. How come?" "Well," Adam said, "you know, God, I discovered I am naked."

Now this is what the play is written for: God said, "Who told thee that thou art naked?" This, to me, is one of the greatest things in the Bible. *Who told thee that thou art naked? Who* told us we were such terrible people, born in sin and conceived in iniquity—and if we are fortunate enough to live for 60 years without dying, or unfortunate enough to live beyond that, it is going to be tough, and after that the deluge. *Who?* This is a concoction of an unconscious sense of guilt being rejected by the Universe and not accepted by It. And I will tell you a good little metaphysical practice to go along with what David has said; I've told it to many people who have a sense of condemnation, because we seem to be born with it out of the collective mind: "Thou, God, approvest of me." *God within me approves of me.*

Any statement that will release the tension of the condemnation without fighting it—in a nonresistant way, in a way that can restore the natural flow . . . and again, in the New Testament John the Baptist is preaching and some poor guy comes along and throws himself face down in the dirt and says, "Sir, what shall I do to escape the wrath to come?" And John looks at him and says, "Look here, guy, get up! I didn't come to tell you what to do to escape the wrath that is to come; I came to tell you that the Kingdom of God is at hand." Now there is a vast difference.

Our theology says the Kingdom of God *is* at hand, that we shall never know any God outside the confines of that only thing which can know anything, whether you call it your conscience or your mind or your awareness —I don't care. It is that thing without which you wouldn't be here; and when it is withdrawn, nothing is left; and what *appears* to be left begins to disintegrate in a split second. The *integrating* factor is "the pearl of great price for which a man will sell everything he has in order that he may possess it": your *self*. Angela Morgan* said, "That inner self that never tires, / Fed by the deep, eternal fires, / Angel and guardian at the gate, / Master of death and king of fate."

I am supposed to be tying religion and psychology together. I know nothing about psychology and very little about religion. Psychology is something there is too much known about which isn't true; religion is something too much is taught about that is false. And yet we need both, because we cannot live without either. One is our perspective of the Cosmos in which we live, and our relationship to what we think is either an overdwelling or an indwelling God. We happen to believe the overdwelling and indwelling God is one God—"The highest God and the innermost God is one God," the mystics say. I put it in a more comprehensive way by saying that God as man in man *is* man—because whatever this Thing is that we call God, It is not an old man with whiskers combing his beard and sending thunderbolts to the Baptists and blessings to the Methodists. There is no such a being, fortunately.

But the Universe is packed full of an equally distributed, undivided, cosmically whole, continually integrated Something that Browning speaks of as "the alive, the awake, and the aware." You find that in the closing of *Saul*, where David has awakened Saul from his apathy and his melancholia as he sings to him: "O Saul, a hand like this hand shall open the gates of new life to thee; see the Christ stand," and the Christ is the Avatar

*New Thought writer and poet.

or the Messiah or the Buddha or the Atman—it is all the same thing: the Son, the Sonship of the Universe. And now *Saul* says, "He slowly resumes his own motions and attitudes. Kingly he is, is Saul; he remembers in glory ere error had bent the broad brow from the daily communion." And then Saul steals quietly out on the desert, and he feels himself surrounded by the alive, the awake, and the aware; and everything speaks to him . . . the stars . . . and then everything sinks to rest and peace. It is the dramatization that Browning gives to the awakening within us of what he called "that spark that disturbs our clod."

Now the Universe in which we live we didn't make; and we will never change it, fortunately. The Ancient of Days is "the same yesterday, today, and forever." But out of Its eternal Being there is an everlasting flow of a forever becoming—"Ever as the spiral grew, / He left the old house for the new." Involuted in that which we are is the seed which gives rise to that which is evoluting out of it, which we shall become. And I was thinking about it the other night and wrote, "The fruit of evolution is in the seed of involution." In our Bible it says—in Genesis— "These are the generations when the plant was made before the seed was in the ground."*

We do not change anything but our reactions to a Universe which acts by some magic of Its own, some mirror, some looking glass—"For life is a mirror of king and slave, / Tis just what you are and do; / Then give to the world the best that you have, / And the best will come

*This is a conflation of Genesis 1:11 (or 12) and 2:4,5.

back to you." Here is the magic mirror of mind, of consciousness or experience or environment—it doesn't matter what we call it—which reflects back to us that which we reflect into it. Mistaking the effect for a cause, we worship the effect, stand in awe of it, not knowing that we are holding it in place by some divine Power which we are not aware of. I call it *divine* because I happen to believe there is nothing but God—in the struggle, in the mistake, in the answer: it is all some of the movement of the original Satchitananda, or divine Bliss.

I happen to believe that everything in the Universe in manifestation exists for the delight of God—not for the glory, as though God were to be glorified; not for our salvation, as though we were lost. All of this is nonsense. It is the babbling of an infant in thought. The Universe exists for the delight of its Creator, that It shall behold Itself in Its own works, know Its beauty in that which is beautiful—and in us, I believe, behold Its beloved Son in whom It is well pleased.

And always there is some reverberation from this shoreless sea of timeless movement underneath which there is absolute silence and stillness. Something I wrote wound up by saying, "Hid within all things evolved, / In silence, beauty, wisdom, will / Is that which makes the cycle move, / Unmoved, immovable, and still." It follows the concept of the Gita and of our Bible and everybody's bible I know about (and I think I have read most of them) that there is involuted, or we are impregnated with, or there is incarnated in us, or however it got there I don't know—there is something in us, an impulsion, a necessity to live, to sing, to dance, to laugh, to love, to come to fruition, and to love creatively. And that life which does not create, or is not lived creatively, creates a surplus of action, now held in the prison within us, beating against the walls of our consciousness for expression.

This is the nature, I think, of the inner conflict—it certainly is very much like that—and the tension and the frustration of the unlived life, and our misinterpretation of the objectification in which we cast the images of our own despair. And we little know something that was illustrated in something I read of a man who had a terrible dream, and he looked up and some awful figure was leaning over his bed, and he was frightened; and he said, "What are you going to do with me?" And the terrible figure leered at him and said, "I am not going to do anything to you; what are *you* going to do to *me*? I am *your* dream, you know." Isn't that terrific? I would like to have made it up!

I was going to say, "back of Dave's simplicity," and that is awful—back of *the doctor's exquisite simplicity*, which is a profundity, it has taken a lifetime of experience and application to come here and tell us the simple things he did. Because *you don't get it out of a book*. It is *in* a man; and then he sits down and as best he can records, as best he may, something that he feels. But words are so inadequate; and it is only when what he feels breathes the words that articulate what is being felt, that the man delivers himself to us and we get what he means. There is no deliverance unless a speaker delivers *himself*—everything that he is. He can talk about love all he wants to —"Isn't it grand? God is Love." But unless his arms are around his audience *literally* as far as they can be *symbolically*—because he loves them—he is not going to get anywhere.

The poet said, "If I had the time to learn from you / How much more comfort my words could do, / And I told you then of my sudden will / To kiss your feet when I did you ill; / If the tears back of the coldness feigned / Could flow, and the wrong be quite explained: / Brothers the souls of us all would chime / —If we had the time." Now this is my religion. It, too, is as simple as David's psychology. It is tied back into the concept of a cosmic Presence incarnated in everything—the bird and the stone and the running brook and the stars and the wind and the wave, the perspiration in the armpits of the laborer.* Whitman said that the prostitute and the libertine, the child sucking at the fountain of Nature from its mother's breast, the man drunk in the gutter, the ascetic, the recluse, and the one in simple adoration all say, "My Lord and my God"; and we shall never find God if we exclude any of these.

You cannot break the Universe into fragments and discover a unitary wholeness in causation, back of some of which might be an illusion and some of which might be real. Bondage is made of freedom, or there is no freedom; unhappiness is made of the possibility of being happy; and Hell will not cool off until we get to Heaven—it is impossible, because the Universe tolerates no otherness, no difference, no fragmentary representation. Everything from the smallest atom to the sidereal universe is forever singing a song of the Cosmos, forever proclaiming the

*Imagery drawn from *Leaves of Grass*, by Walt Whitman.

presence of That which is complete. We feel it by some subtle mystical, inner sense, and I doubt not that all of our trouble, just as Doctor Fink has said, is a result of our frustrations, which inhibit its flow—because everything is in a flow in the Universe; it is a liquidity; it is what is always called, or likened to, water—the primordial substance from which the mundane universe emanated. It is just a symbol.

Now then: if these things are true, and if what David said is true—and I do not doubt that they are true—there is only one little guy that we really have to work with, isn't there? "God and I in space alone, / And nobody else in view; / 'And where are the people, God,' I said, / And the dead whom once I knew?' / 'There are no people,' the great God said; / 'No earth beneath or sky o'erhead. / There is nothing at all but you.'" Now this isn't solecism. This is true. Every reaction we have to life is the reaction of what we are to the life with which we must live—the people with whom we are associated. What do we see? What do we hear? What is our reaction? "Well," we might say, "what has all this to do with religion?" Well, religion is a life. You know, people can pray until they get so frustrated they are crazy—because unless the prayer looses a frustration, it will just make it worse. I guess I should take this back; but it is true.

I happen to know someone who is one of the most brilliant women in America—was having lunch with her not long ago—and she was cussing things out pretty much in general. And I said, "This is a strange thing to me; why do you suppose it is that you have so much self-condemnation?" She was just about to crown me with the sugar bowl; she said, "I do *not* have condemnation for myself!"

I said, "This is all you have talked about. You are projecting yourself. You are like a person who has stopped
drinking coffee and says, 'Nobody else shall ever drink
coffee again; it is wrong—because *I* have stopped.'" I
said, "Way back in your mind you have the most terrific
sense of having been cast out of Heaven as most anybody
I know of." She said, "This is hard to believe." "But," I
said, "this is true. 'Thou doest protest too loudly.'"

Now *we* are the only guy who has to come clean; and
I don't believe we will ever do it until we get better
acquainted with whatever this Thing is that we call God
—whatever this Thing is that we call ourselves. It won't
be through *a false egotism*; it will be *a certain egoism*
in the sense that we shall have to respect the fact that,
as Emerson said, if God hadn't had need of you, He
wouldn't have put you here. You are an organ of the
Infinite.

I think we have every right to intelligently recognize
whether we say we are Sons of the living God or whatever we choose to call It. We are the offspring of a Universe that at least saw fit to give birth to us—and I don't
believe God makes any mistakes; there can be no mistakes in the divine Plan. (*We* have plenty of them!)

I think a certain amount of meditation, prayer, contemplation reaches that Secret Place of the Most High.
Believe me, I tried it last week because I felt I had some
things I had to get straightened up, and I went away for
six days all by myself and I talked to myself on an average of ten hours a day—because I knew I needed it—and
it happened.

Now *what* happened? There is nothing that *could* have
happened other than that the frustration was removed

long enough for some Light to come through. "There is a Light that lighteth every man's path"; there is a Silence at the center of every person that speaks; there is a Word that is heard; there is a Presence that is felt; there is a Power that flows; and a Peace. It comes out of some eternal Stillness—so still that the Silence becomes articulate. Now I know it; because whenever I get where I think I need that, that is what I do. Now what happens? I think in a sense it is like boring a tunnel until it hits the reservoir and a clearance is made and out gushes the water, as Moses struck the rock with a rod. Because the water is always there. "He has not left Himself without a witness."

Now we practice the Science of Mind, spiritual mind healing, and we believe in it. We are the first group of metaphysicians who have ever deliberately set about, as I did 30 years ago,* to build a bridge between metaphysics, science, philosophy, religion, medicine, psychology, and psychiatry. I have been at it for 30 years, and I hope it won't take another 30 years. We are well on the way. It shouldn't have to happen that way, because the world is going to need every good that is at its disposal. Therefore you become practitioners.

To feel that disease or poverty is some terrible evil or some awful thing imposed on us, or to lay too much stress on our own error . . . the psychiatrist has a little more charity than most religionists: he knows it is the neurosis talking and not the neurotic, and he separates the belief from the believer. We have to separate what

---

*I.e. 1927. This marks the formal beginnings of Religious Science. But Ernest Holmes had been working on his "bridge" long before that.

is human from the divine, and we have to have confidence enough to believe that we are a witness to some infinite Beauty. But how shall we be a witness to that which we have not witnessed? How shall we speak that which we have not heard? How shall we know that which we have not seen, and how shall we think that which we have not conceived? We shall not.

Most of your practice won't be with what objectively it looks as though it were about; not even the people. It will be with *yourself*; because all they are going to get from you is *yourself*. They can't get anything else. As Theodore Reik* said in his book *Listening with the Third Ear*: there is a third ear that must listen, and an artistry about psychiatric analytical work; and if a person doesn't listen with a third ear and doesn't have that intuition developed, he will not do very much with his patients.

It is an understanding heart, a seeing eye; it is a something that feels back through all this apparent ugliness, this strange confusion, as Riley† said, "in that mad race where none achieve," and finds in itself that which it may now uncover in another. And believe me, such people heal those around them without any thought at all. Something is transmitted. As Whittier‡ said, "The healing of the seamless dress / Is but by our beds of pain; / We touch Him in life's strong embrace, / And we are whole again."

No psychiatrist and no metaphysician is ever going to make anybody else any more whole than he is himself.

---

*(1888–1969), Austrian-American psychoanalyst and author.
†James Whitcomb Riley (1849–1916), American poet.
‡John Greenleaf Whittier (1807–1892), American poet.

It is impossible. If the blind lead the blind, they will both fall into the ditch. It is something that David has learned and that field is beginning to learn, and it will hook onto religion some day—but, we shall hope, a religion without superstition; because religion with superstition is better than none, but it isn't as good as it could be.

Religion is a life—a feeling we have to the Universe. It is a way of thinking and acting. It is a secret we have with each other. It is something that reveals us to each other in love, in purity—and I am not speaking of purity in the ethical sense; I am speaking of the *pure sacrifice,* where the reality stands out—where we have nothing to sell and do not wish to buy anything; and where we live a life which I believe no one can tell us much about, other than to say, "This is the Way." I believe everyone will have to find the most of it; that is why we never give formulas. David didn't give a formula. He said, "Practice this kind of a thing and that kind of a thing." Because why? Every time you give a treatment, every time you pray, every time you talk about something, you never do the same thing twice alike.

You know, if a river is the same river it was yesterday, and stays so, and you should drink from it, in a few days it would poison you. It is only in the movement and the flow, from the mountaintops of your inspiration and adoration, that there is an imbibing that is cosmic. And so we can never do the same thing twice alike, or pray the same prayer. That is why there are no formulas. Something new, something spontaneous, something in my estimation that never happened in all the Universe before happens every time somebody takes a picture. Or as Emerson said, "The Ancient of Days is in the latest invention." It is *here*. He said we should say, not God *spake*, but *speaks*; not God *was*, but *is*. This *is* the beloved Son, which Son you are.

And so we tie this whole thing back into a sort of mystical—not mysterious—sense of our relationship to Something which is very beautiful, Something which is very still inside of us. Emerson said of the Lady of the Lake: "She is calm and, whatsoever storms assail the sea, and when the tempest rolls, hath power to walk the waters like our Lord."

Now there are people wouldn't understand what we are talking about—would think we are crazy and all that. They said that about Socrates and Jesus—not that I am likening myself to them; but what they discovered is what we are in search of. And if as great a man as Socrates could laugh while Plato was crying and say, "Plato thinks *this* is Socrates"; and if Jesus could say, "It is expedient that I go away in order that the Spirit of Truth may bear witness to the Fact I have taught you"; and if he can say to the thief on the cross beside him, "Today shalt thou be with me in paradise"; and if we companion with the great and the good and commune with their thoughts through their written words until we enter into a psychic consciousness that isn't written at all, in my estimation (I am sure of it; that is why we read great literature, that is why we listen to great music: it is what *wasn't* recorded that is suggested by what *was*; and I believe it is transcendent) . . . if these great people could do this, so can we—you and I—with a humility that is not false, a simplicity that is direct, a claim upon the Universe where the soul makes its great claim on God that is not arrogance.

I don't think we should be afraid. I think the beginning of wisdom is not the fear of God but the knowledge, the love, the worship, the adoration, the sense of a divine Presence. As Emerson said, "How wonderful is the thought of God peopling the lonely places with His presence." And it is only when we become lonely enough that That which is Alone in us gropes out and finds the Alone in other things, and the loneliness is gone.

Alone to the Alone, the One to the One, the Only to the Only. We shall never successfully practice our Science unless we do spend much time seeking that Thing within us which is beyond fear, beyond isolation, beyond separation, beyond good and evil, beyond what theology teaches—that simplicity, that childlikeness which is not child*ish* but is child*like*: this is the essence of religion; "But what am I?; / An infant crying in the night; / An infant crying for the light; / And with no language but a cry." "But the feeble hands and helpless, / Groping blindly in the darkness, / Touched God's right hand in that darkness / And are lifted up and strengthened."

This no living soul can do for you nor for me. But hid deep within the soul, hid deep within the silence, hid in the beauty of Nature, is That which speaks. And the bush burns, and the ground becomes hallowed and the spot sacred; and That is you, and That is myself. That is each other; That is the whole world. And if the materialists shall scoff at it, we are not concerned; if someone shall criticize it, we are not dismayed; if someone shall say such things are not—we shall not listen. There is a testimony of the soul, there is an inward awareness, which you shall discover. And then you shall meet God in yourself.

91

CHAPTER 6

This Thing Called Life

In March of 1958 Dr. Ernest Holmes went to Florida to speak in Fort Lauderdale, St. Petersburg, Orlando, and Miami. The last talk of this series was given in Miami on March 26th. He selected the title of his favorite book, *This Thing Called Life*, as his topic for the evening.

T HIS BRIEF SERIES of talks will come to a close tonight. I have so much enjoyed being here and talking with you. I never talk *to* people or *at* people. Our work is a sort of counseling together to try to find out what it is we believe, why we believe it, whether or not we think it makes sense, and whether it will work. For we have no platitudes, we have no formulas, and we have no sweet sayings. If we did, I wouldn't be here. Nor would anybody else. Religious Science in essence is not anything new in the world. In *action* it *is* new. It's a putting together the highlights of the thoughts of the ages and seeing what they add up to; and it is an attempt also to use these thoughts and embody their meaning for life. It's a life— it's a *living*—based upon the best that the world knows.

It's been very wonderful, the response we've had these two weeks here—Ft. Lauderdale, St. Petersburg, and Orlando. I don't know where all the people came from. It shows what a great vitality must exist in the idea that you and I believe in. It also shows that the world is ready for something perhaps a little different—not necessarily better, but different. The world is certainly waiting for some sign, I happen to believe (it's only my opinion), whether or not it knows or recognizes the fact—the world is waiting for definite and concrete evidence of the reality of the hope that springs perennial in the human breast. For whether or not we know or are aware of the fact, every man's life individually, and therefore all men's lives collectively, are, in the last analysis, more influenced by their thoughts of God or their belief in some supreme Power than anything else.

Now that will include every religion. This is why religion and art are the two oldest institutions in the world, and the only two institutions that have come down through the ages and not been destroyed by pestilence, tidal wave, time, revolution, or the forming and dissolution of empires. Always these two institutions have stood as though they were silent watchers over the evolution of humanity. And religion and art are intuitive perceptions of the nature of the Universe in which we live. They are a feeling toward and for the invisible.

And so I chose the subject "This Thing Called Life." I wrote a book, *This Thing Called Life*, which is one of the biggest sellers that ever appeared in this field. I deliberately chose to call it "This Thing Called Life" rather than "Jehovah" or "Buddha" or "Allah" or "the Absolute." As I was thinking of a name, a friend of mine said, "I have a title for you, but I don't think I want to give it to you." I said, "What is it?" and he said, "This Thing Called Life." I said "You don't have to give it to me—I have already taken it!"—a very wonderful title, because it calls the unknown *Life*: This Thing Called *Life*.

Now life is the thing that eludes us. All the biologists in the world do not know what life is; all the psychologists do not know what the mind is. They are merely among the watchers of the action of either an unknown Guest or an unknown Host, and no one knows exactly which—that Thing which we call God, which animates everything and makes everything what it is, and without which nothing would be. I chose to call it "This Thing Called Life" because I wanted to keep the theological connotation or implication away from it.

I discovered a very charming cousin of mine here in your very wonderful, very beautiful city, and she asked me the difference between religion and theology. I told her religion is our faith in God; theology is the dogma that grows up around it that finally people come to believe is so because people believed in it. But religion itself is native to the soul. A person without a religion is not wide awake intellectually, emotionally, or spiritually.

Religion is essential to the mind, because it is impossible for any person to feel that he must single-handed and alone combat the Universe. There is a gravitational force that's holding this watch in place, this desk, this building, and the whole universe, and we do not have to help it. It is something that operates automatically. We work so hard, Jesus said, "for the meat that perisheth," and we struggle so hard to do things by pushing and pulling and shoving and hauling, as Lowell said:

Bubbles we earn with a whole soul's tasking;
'Tis heaven alone that is given away,
'Tis only God may be had for the asking.

Now Life exists. Nothing is more certain. Life is intelligent; It responds to us. We happen to believe It's a spiritual Presence, everywhere equally distributed, and within us and around us, and everywhere else. Life—call It God, call It anything you want to: there is Something present with us and in us, out of whose essence all things are made, within whose creative imagination all things are formed, and by whose inexorable and immutable laws all things are held in place. This is self-evident. Here we are, and we couldn't be here if these things were not true.

This Thing called Life—now what has it to do with the human personality? This Thing called Life *is* the human personality. Just as we have not seen God, we have not seen each other. We think that we have seen each other, but we haven't. We have seen the objective manifestation of something that's impelled and propelled by an invisible awareness which is the real self. Angela Morgan said:

That inner self you have not known,
Looking on flesh and blood alone—
That inner self that never tires,
Fed by the deep eternal fires,
Angel and guardian at the gate,
Master of death and king of fate.

Now there *is* such a self—there isn't any question about it. There is the self that no one has ever plumbed. The

more deeply psychology plumbs what it calls the unconscious, or some of the deeper aspects of this self, the more
it finds it still has not reached. There is always more.
The Bible speaks of it as a river whose source no man
has seen.

There is a flowing into each one of us, in my estimation, a unique presentation of the Universe itself; and
every man is a center in a Consciousness which is Itself
universal or cosmic, all-encompassing, endless, forever
expansive. We are all in the process of an eternal evolution, destined to be ever more and never less ourselves.
Every man is in the pathway of unfoldment. That there
must be endless entities, beings, beyond us as we are
beyond tadpoles, I am completely convinced.

Now this is something that we ought to believe in and
realize, because what we think about we become; what
we believe and accept becomes a part of our being. Our
consciousness and its awareness constitute the only absolutely solid, sole, evidence of being there is; because if
you were to take consciousness away, there would be
nothing left. That this consciousness of yours and mine
extends out or in—or perhaps both out *and* in—to some
limitless infinitude, I do not know. How else are you
going to account for a man like Mahatma Gandhi in
modern times, a Buddha in his time, or Moses or Jesus or
any of the other great spiritual geniuses? Gandhi would
sit there, and a million persons who couldn't possibly
hear his voice (and didn't have to; it didn't matter
whether he spoke or not) became enraptured as they
gradually merged into the influence of whatever we may
call it; they call it *darshan* in India. It means that this
thing is established between people, as whatever it is in

one and whatever it is in the other meet in a third place in space. I have always known that it happens betwen an audience and a speaker. It's one of the first things I ever discovered. It is the consciousness of the audience and the consciousness of the speaker meeting, and then flowing back into each other, and adding something greater than either one could have done of himself or itself.

Now that some spiritual awareness, some interior awareness, some transcendent something emanated from Gandhi and Jesus and many others there is no question at all. As a matter of fact, this influence is exercised on all planes—material, mental, physical, spiritual, esthetic, artistic—and we feel people, we feel atmospheres. We little realize what they are. As Emerson said, "What you are speaks so loudly I cannot hear what you are saying." Shakespeare said, "My words fly up, my thoughts remain below: / Words without thoughts, never to Heaven go." Here is something that you cannot measure. I do not know what it is. Loosely, let us call it the personality, the ego, individuality, the Thing Itself, that which Life is in us; because I believe there is only one Life Principle. God is One. "Hear, O Israel: the Eternal, the Lord thy God is one God." I believe that there is only one Spirit in the Universe. "There is one mind common to all men," Emerson said.

I happen to believe that we live by the Spirit of God, we think because the mind of God is in us, and we expand because we expand from the finite into the Infinite. You cannot contract the Infinite, you *can* expand the finite. We may all expand more and more and yet more, and I believe forever, here and then somewhere else. I have no worry about shucking off this mortal coil. Someone said to me the other day, "You certainly don't believe every-body goes to the same place, do you?" Fortunately, God is taking care of that. I said I would ask him one thing and he could answer it. I said, "Did we all arrive at the same place when we got here?" and he said, "Yes." I said, "You've answered your own question."

There is no reason in the world why you and I should be soul-savers—because, believe me, my friends: if I am lost, there is no one else who will know where to find me. Now that is nothing against the Miamians; if we were in Los Angeles I'd say the same thing. *There is nothing lost.* But certain things in our mental and spiritual anatomy at times seem slightly misplaced. We can almost lose hope. But Truth will rise again. There is a side of us which lies open to the Infinite; then as it comes down and flows through us, it influences people—not because we try to make it; we don't want it to, in that sense.

We do not teach how to influence people, how to get rich, how to have one of those dominating personalities. That is very silly. There are lots of people who actually believe that there is someone who *can* teach them. There is no such thing. Every man is an institution in his own right, and "Every institution is the length and shadow of somebody's thought," Emerson said. Every person is already equipped with everything he can need or he wouldn't be here. God never makes mistakes; and so I happen to believe that right back of me and right back of you, and within us, there is a unique individualization of Eternity itself, of the whole Thing. No two persons are alike. As Emerson said, "Imitation is suicide."

Now suppose there were at the center of the being of each one of us a clear channel to the Infinite, which is forever pouring out through us in a unique way, because it never does two things alike, nor does it ever repeat itself. Somewhere at the center of our being, should we properly use it, would be that thing we would all like to be, which is certain to be happy and well and prosperous, successful; it is certain to be established in peace, to experience joy, to know life; it is certain, if it is understood and permitted and cultivated, to bless everything that it touches. This would be our influence on our environment; it wouldn't be an influence that dominates people, or controls them, but it would be an influence that would irresistibly bring back from most people a very great affection, a very great love. People are lonely, you know.

One of the greatest needs in the world is to heal the loneliness of the human mind; people feel very much alone and are unhappy and insecure. Now I can't imagine any person being lonely very long who could come to comprehend the meaning of the divine presence of the living, creative Spirit incarnated in himself and one with all other people, because if he consciously practiced this, he would have more friends than he would have time for, objectively. In other words, his inward awareness automatically would attract to him that which is like that awareness.

Anyone who truly loves people will be loved by people. Anyone who has healed himself of the hurt of life will find countless numbers of people gathering around him that they may be healed too, as Whittier said: "The healing of the seamless vest / Is by our beds of pain. / We touch him in life's throng and press, / And we are whole again." Now I know there are a lot of people who study to influence people and make friends, and be superduper salesmen. That is not the way the Universe is organized. Who told God how to be God? Who told the nightingale how to sing? Who told the chicken how to lay an egg?

You know, the story of Job in the old Testament is an example of this. He was a good man; but it seemed as though there were great visitations of misfortune upon him. He lost everything he had—his family and his horses and his cattle; and he had three friends and a wife who comforted him, or tried to, and they told him he had probably been bad, and he said he thought he had been good and done everything. Finally, he had to discharge his three counselors (Job's comforters). Then Mama Job says, "Well, Papa, there is nothing left but to curse God and to die." He said, "I think you are wrong. There is an integrity in me, and in my integrity shall I see God." Now this is just a story and it is a good one.

And Job told God he'd done everything: he hadn't muzzled the oxen when they threshed the grain, and he'd left grain in the fields for the gleaners; he had given his tithes to the temple and much more; he had entertained his friends and the alien within his gates, he had been good to his family, he had worshiped God; and so he was complaining and sort of setting himself up as the only cause that there was.

So in the argument God finally said, "Well, Job, you have done very well, and I have watched you, and I have admired you; but there are some things you don't happen to be aware of. Where were you when I set the stars in their course and started the North Wind? I just don't remember seeing you around, Job." And for the first time Job realized—and this is the meaning of the story—that you and I take it out. We don't put it in; *we take it out.*

It's already there. So he falls down and says, "I see now how it is: I have interfered with the divine operation of the cosmic Law." And it was then that everything was restored to him, as it would have to be.

This is a story, written by a man with a very dramatic, creative imagination, to teach a cosmic truth as he saw it.

You and I do not hold things in place; we are operated upon—not only by physical laws that are cosmic, like gravitational force, fractional repulsion, cohesion. *All* the laws and forces of Nature act upon us. We are acted upon by great mental and spiritual laws in the same way, and the final law of our whole being is the law of our acceptance or rejection of Life itself. Do we or do we not believe? Are we alone buffeted by fate? Are we persecuted by the vicissitudes of fortune? Have both God and man denied us the right to be happy? So many entertain this psychological and emotional attitude and blame everybody for everything.

And so we have to reverse this, come to an inner awareness. And there is no final psychological or physiological or psychosomatic clearance until spiritual realization changes the imagery of our imagination, that in its place it may react on the body and the environment, which are but reflections cast into the mirror of some medium that acts like a reflector to bring back to the thinker the objectification of his thoughts.

Now there is no willpower, none of this terrific thing. If a person can love enough, he will be loved; there won't be any question about it. If he has entered a state of peace in his own mind, people will feel peaceful around him and want to be there. If he sees that he is one with the great human race, he will have more friends than he can attend to. But even though this should be a hope in his mind, an anguish, a longing covertly expressed, even expressed in the Holy of Holies through prayer and supplication, and he himself did not believe his own entreaty: it would be as though it had not been heard; and this is something people don't understand. They say, "Why has God done this to me?" "Why has life done this to me?"

It is very difficult for any of us to understand that the nature of the Universe is such whether we like it or do not like it; that until we affirmatively comply with Its affirmation, even Its affirmation shall appear to us as a negation, by the same word in reverse, just as heat will burn us, cook our food, explode and burn down the building, or warm our hands and feet—just as perhaps the electrical energy that toasts the Pope's bread is the one that will kill a criminal that is being electrocuted. The great forces of nature are impartial and impersonal.

Now it so happens in our philosophy of this Thing called Life, we believe that we are one with all the Power there is. We are not that Power; we are one with It. We are one with all the Life there is. We are not that Life; It is what we are. We are a cast of the only Mind and the only creative Imagination there is. It's all here, and we have to believe it, because if we don't believe it, we believe it *isn't*. Therefore there must be an acceptance.

There's a big difference in the attitude, when I get up in the morning, if I say it's a bad day, it's a tough day, etc.—or if I say, "Good morning, God!" *That's* quite a different attitude—the attitude of a child. "The sun is lovely; thank you, God. I'm glad to be alive!" There's a very great difference how we start the day. One may say, "I wonder what rascal I'll meet, and I wonder who is going to do me in today." Now this is an attitude, and it's anybody's privilege to assume it. But there must be a government of Law in the Universe. Browning said, "All's love and yet all's law." And he was right. Then another may say, "This is the day God has made. I'm going to be glad in it. I live and exist on the threshold of opportunity. Every person I meet shall be blessed and helped; and there is a deep and abiding peace in me which shall be transmitted to everyone I meet." What a difference in these attitudes!

And now we know what mental attitudes do. They brush off on people. Personality brushes off like feathers, and everybody feels it. If we are psychically antagonistic, everyone feels it, and they feel ruffled up. They don't know why, but if we shake their hands they would like to shove us away. But if there is the all-embracing heart, even as they shake our hand with one hand, they try to get the other hand around us. It's irresistible. Now, this doesn't happen by chance. It isn't just saying, "Jesus loves me, this I know, for the Bible tells me so." That's sweet, but *this* ain't *that*.

There's something very dynamic about this, something terrific. There's something that works with mathematical accuracy and immutable certainty. Nothing can change it. It is a law in the Universe. Because we all live in the One Mind, we all live in the One Power and the One Presence. If we learn to see in each other that which we would like to be, we shall much quicker become that which we would like to be—because a house divided against itself cannot stand.

There's no such thing as my having the slightest little bit of salvation. (I hate to use the word because I don't believe in it; we're not lost. But you know what I mean.) We can't have the slightest little bit at all. The Universe will have no exclusions. Over the doorway of the Kingdom of Holiness has indelibly been imprinted the word *Others*, always. Why is that? Because each one of us is a center in the consciousness of the Whole and in the consciousness of each other. And remember this: the life that includes the most is the biggest.

So we would like to have wonderful personalities. People say, "Can't somebody come and give us a class on the development of personality?" If you know anyone who can give you a class on how to lay an egg, that's grand, and you settle with him; and I'll bet anything if it hatches, it's a rotten egg. It won't hatch. It just isn't that way. If it were that way, then a man who could hold thoughts the hardest without getting crosseyed, and the man who could concentrate the most without getting a headache, would govern everybody else. History proves the reverse. Only the lovers of humanity have been loved by it.

But we measure things by a pretty short distance, don't we? Too short, in fact. Here in eternal Existence we can measure them only by the long reach and the great outsweep of time. It already has a way of finally dissipating everything that is negative and bringing forward the great affirmations, because that's the way It lives. It's the way God says, "I am; and that also I am, beside which there is none other."

Now this thing works automatically. A life that really loves people will be loved. But it's got to be *real*. It can't be done as a trick—even a metaphysical one—and it can't be done as a sweet affirmation, saying, "I love you, even though you are a stinker." It isn't that way at all.

Love only knows and comprehendeth love. It is true. It is all-inclusive, and in such degree as that happens to one's own soul, he will be embraced by humanity. I know it. Very, very few people have ever had as much love as I have had, and I love people, good, bad and indifferent —because we are all indifferent anyway. We're all partly good and we're all partly—not *bad*, but just a little *loose* here and there, this way and that way; and that's all right. It's the set of the sail and not the gale that we must pay attention to.

We all have an inward longing, an irresistible desire to embrace the Universe, and so often we are afraid of it. Don't be afraid of that. It is only the one who abandons himself to the genius of this Thing called Life that could ever hope to have that Thing articulate itself through him. What is It but that Thing that wrote every song, and dances every dance; what is It but that Artist who painted every picture. And that is why the poet said, "When earth's last picture is painted / And the views are twisted and dried, / And the oldest color is faded / And the youngest critic has died— / We shall rest."

Now it so happens, in my belief, that each one of us is an institution in the Universe—unique, entirely new, will never be reproduced. But don't we sit around saying, "I don't know. I haven't got it. I haven't the looks, the talent, the brains or spiritual equipment"—? And in our field they say, "I don't have enough understanding, and I'm not spiritual enough." It's all nonsense; it's all a part of that strange unconscious self-condemnation that man seems to bedevil himself with through life.

I have never known a man, and never shall, who, having cleared himself first of this condemnation of his own being, will ever judge another. It's only a projection. It's why Jesus said, "Judge not that ye be not judged, for with what judgment ye judge, ye shall be judged, and with what measure ye mete, it shall be measured to you again." That's not a platitude. All Jesus was saying, if he had said it in another way, would be this: "Water will reach its own level by its own weight"; and you don't force it. Let someone get a clearance in his own mind from ugliness, and everything shall be beautiful to him.

I had a funeral not long ago, because of a mutual friend. I did not know the people or this elderly lady who had passed on, didn't see any members of the family. I sat there while the song was being sung, and I thought, "Now look here, something in me knows about this person. There is some part of me that always knew her and embraced her." So when I got up to talk, I didn't talk much about immortality. All I could talk about was *beauty*, and I did it for 20 minutes. So after it was over, two sons came to me and said, "Oh, that was terrific!" I said, "Let me ask you something: was your mother an artist?" and one of them said, "No, not in the ordinary sense; but her whole life was a work of art and a thing of beauty, and had you known her all her life, you could not have said it any better."

What was the thing I felt? It is what she was, it's the memory left behind, it's the feeling that these things go through life with us, and people feel them and they know them and they will embrace or reject us according to whether or not we are embracing or rejecting the Universe itself. And suppose we include joy and beauty and love and faith—all of these attitudes are contagious.

I read not long ago in a popular magazine about a man who got on a streetcar and was whistling and having a wonderful time on his way to work. He sat down beside somebody and had to be there for half an hour, but before the half hour was over he wished he could go out and kill himself. This man beside him was in a very melancholy and almost desperate emotional state, and this just transmitted itself to him. He couldn't understand why he felt that way. There is something about us that rubs off, definitely.

We looked at the picture of Lowell Thomas* and his son, their travel to Tibet last summer; and here always the prayers and prayer wheel, praying, praying, appeasing the devils and evil influences, the hills and bad spirits of the canyons, and exorcising the spirits of the water before they could cross the flowing river where the water is very swift. How silly; yet is that any different from what we do in our theology? We think that is very crude, don't we? Yet it isn't one bit more crude than what 90 percent of the people do, each in his own language. And that's all wrong.

What kind of a God are we proclaiming, what kind of This Thing Called Life? Seems to me we should be filled with joy and happiness. Dare to be yourself; you have nothing else. That thing which the Infinite and Almighty has endowed each one of us with we have rejected because it is so simple, so unassuming. "How could it be me? It must be some great character, some great figure in history; it must be some saviour, some Christ or

*(1892–1981), American traveler, journalist, and author.

Buddha." No, *they* did it for *themselves*; and they did well. Therefore they become great wayshowers—not saviours.

Nothing can save us but ourselves; nothing can bring peace and quiet but our own consciousness; nothing can bless the world, so far as you and I are concerned, but you and I. God has already blessed it, and if it were not so, we would all be living by proxy. The greatest thing that can happen to any living soul is finally to learn to take himself for better or worse; to say, "I am this that I am—good, bad, or indifferent. From this point, I must go forward." "Sun across its course may go, / The Ancient river still may flow, / And I am still *I am*."

And, as one thinks long and deeply, silently within himself, and listens, something happens to him. There is a witness to the soul—irrefutable, irrevocable, absolutely certain. The only prophetic thing that can ever happen to you and to me, is not to read—just read—what others have done, but somehow or other, taking that as an example, to do the same thing.

Now we would like this dynamic personality.

We've got it. But we aren't using it—that's all.

We would like this creative something. *We have it.* But we're not using it.

The key to the Kingdom of God was locked in the Secret Place of the Most High, in the heart of every living soul before ever time began. It's predetermined, it's predestined. It's written in the constitution and nature of the Universe that you and I and everyone else is the beloved Son, and as Eckhart said, "God is forever begetting His Only-Begotten, and He is begetting Him in me now." What a wonderful possibility!

When at long last we have laid down the burden and the struggle and the doubt and the fear and the uncertainty and the questioning "Where shall I go, and what shall I do, to be saved?" at last some sweet clarion call as as from the pipe of Pan shall cause the Sun to stand still. "Sweet, sweet, O Pan—piercing sweet"; by the river is that clarion call blown by your own lips echoing evermore, "This is my beloved Son"; "I am that which Thou art, Thou art that which I am." Wonderful the ears that can hear the message of the saints and sages who proclaim not unto us but unto Thee. Enlightened is the one who at long last, sitting in the silence of his own soul, shall no longer be afraid to say, "Good morning, God!"

CHAPTER 7

The Power of an Idea

Dr. Holmes repeated many times that "thoughts are things."
He stressed *the power of an idea*. The preceding Miami talk
was still in his thinking when he returned to Los Angeles
in April 1958, and on Sunday the 27th he delivered this talk
on the Power of an Idea at the Wiltern Theater. For what these
two talks contained—indeed, for their very strong content—
I labeled this entire volume of *The Holmes Papers* "Ideas
of Power."

IN THE SCRIPTURE reading George* read this morning,
it says, "In the beginning was the Word, and the Word
was with God, and the Word was God. And all things
were made by the Word; and without the Word was not
anything made that was made. And the Word became
flesh and dwelt among us, and we beheld It." The Bible
and all bibles—because ours is one of many—all start
with the proposition that there is one Life, one Mind, one
Intelligence, one Law, and that everything proceeds from

*George Bendall.

this One, and everything lives in this One. Everything lives by It.

Dr. Bill* is back in New York with the Guru of India.† He is to the Hindu world what the Pope is to the Christian world: countless millions of people look to him as their spiritual guide. This is the first time in a thousand years that a man in his office has ever left India. He became very fond of Bill when he was here. He is one of the great spiritual lights of the world. It is a very great honor for Bill and for us that he should insist on seeing Bill before he embarks for India, nor could we have a better ambassador than Dr. Bill. We are very proud he had this invitation, is on this mission, and our thought and word and love are with him, as his are with us; and we shall struggle along and do the best we can. Bill is a great ambassador anywhere.

"In the beginning was the Word." All the bibles of the world teach that everything in Creation is a result of the divine Spirit—God, Jehovah, Brahma, the Absolute, the Reality; doesn't matter what you call It—operating upon Itself, and out of this Self making that which still is Itself. "Who hath seen me hath seen the Father." This is the very foundation of our philosophy: God is all there is.

When we use the word *God*, we mean the Cause, the invisible Intelligence, the Divinity, that omnipresent Knowingness; Spirit, Life, Truth, Reality—that is what

*William Hornaday.
†Sri Shankaracharya Bharati Krishna Tirtha of Puri, India—senior head of the Swami Order.

111

we mean by God. And when we say that God is everywhere, we mean that God is in us, in each other, in this
flower, in the interspaces of the universe. *There is nothing but God*. Anything that denies this divine Presence is
an illusion. It is a false conclusion.

God is all there is. "I am that I am beside which there
is none other." There is God, Spirit, Life and nothing out
of which to make everything.* Therefore everything is
God, and God in manifestation. And though I read lately,
much to my surprise but not horror, that Hell has recently been moved from New York to San Francisco, I
still don't believe in it. A state of consciousness has traveled across the country and, I would say, a doleful one.

Everything is made up of an idea. Our ideas are either
false or else they are true. The false idea has never created
the truth, and the true idea has never been disturbed by
the false. Or, as the Bhagavad Gita says (and that is the
book, next to the New Testament, which is read the most
in the world, and has been for hundreds of years; it is
the book Gandhi read every day; a universal Truth), the
Truth has never ceased to be, the Real has never ceased
to be; the unreal never has been.

It is our philosophy that if we scrape away the debris
—that which contradicts the divine Presence—we shall
find a Divinity concealed in everything, every person,
everywhere, all the time. It is our belief that in such

*This thought is expressed more fully in Dr. Holmes' *The Science of
Mind*: "There is Spirit—or this Invisible Cause—and nothing, out
of which all things are to be made. Now, Spirit plus nothing leaves
Spirit only. Hence there is One Original Cause and nothing, out of
which we are made. In other words, we are made from this Thing"
(p. 36).

degree as we may individually and collectively perceive this Divinity, It will appear. "Act as though I am, and I will be."

There is Something in everything and in every person that responds to this recognition, this penetration, this beholding in each other truth, beauty, love, reason, gladness, joy; responds to seeing It in our environment. And to see It in our surroundings is to call It forth as though we recognized Something which knew Its own name. "Look unto me and be ye saved, all the ends of the earth."

It is our belief—that is why we are here—that every man is "a God though in the germ." That is what Browning meant in "Rabbi Ben Ezra" where he said, "I shall thereupon / Take rest, ere I be gone / On my adventure brave and new, / Fearless and unperplexed / When I wage battle next, / What weapons to select, / What armour to endue. / Fool! All that is, at all, / Lasts forever, past recall; / Earth changes, but thy soul and God stand sure: / What entered into thee / That was, is, and shall be: / Time's wheel runs back or stops: Potter and clay endure." There is nothing but God. God is infinite Intelligence. The Word of God, the Thought of God, the Idea of God is the *Action* of God. As St. Augustine said, it was very evident that the creative Word was the contemplation of God—He didn't use crowbars or levers —and every scripture tells us that Creation is the result of the contemplation of the Self-knowingness of God.

Now by contemplation we mean that with which God is identified. For instance, we want to think about peace: it is an idea to begin with, it is a thought; we say "peace" and we begin to get a little more peaceful. We meditate upon the idea of peace; we get into the idea of peace, a deeper sense of peace; we identify ourselves with peace: "I am that which Thou art"—peace within my soul; "Thou art that which I am"—infinite peace within me. There is nothing but peace. Now *this* is identifying with peace!

And as we do, we think the idea "peace." Plato said everything is made up of divine ideas—that is what he meant: the thoughts of God; "In the beginning was the Word." God thought Creation into existence and is still thinking it into existence in you and in me. The creative Energy and Intelligence that speaks the planets into their spheres of rotation and revolution is the same Intelligence that digests our food and enables us to read the morning paper—if we can find anything in it.

"In the beginning was the Word"; and *this* is the beginning, because you never can step into the same river twice. The only thing that is permanent is change, but within it is that which identifies it. Now that is true. It is also true that that which we contemplate and identify ourselves with we will attract to us; we shall be attracted to it. Now that is one of our troubles, theoretically. All of us should be well, happy, prosperous, radiant, filled with joy and enthusiasm.

I talked to a woman the other day and she said, "I have this certain physical trouble"—which included a wrong blood pressure and wrong lots of things—"and yet the doctor says there is no reason why I should have to have it: I ought to be well." I talked to her awhile and treated her—and I said, "I'll tell you your trouble, my dear; and you don't have to accept it." I said, "Your trouble is a lack of an enthusiastic interest in life—and of giving yourself to some form of expression which expresses you."

"Well," she said, "it's a funny thing, but that is what

my doctor told me." She said, "What shall I do?" and I asked, "What *did* you do?" She said, "I used to play the piano all the time, teaching." So I said, "Get out your old piano and begin to play it." She said, "I couldn't teach any more"; and I said, "How do you know you can't?" She made all kinds of excuses: fingers too stiff, can't play any more, etc.

I said, "You have stopped living but not dropped dead. Life and action are the same thing. It is now known in medicine and accepted that where there is this continued ennui and lack of physical vitality, even when there is no real particular infection or reason for illness, any doctor will tell you the illness is because people lack an enthusiastic zest for life. The child has gone out of them —the wonder, the merriment, the joy."

"And he took a child and stood him in their midst and said, Suffer the little children to come unto me and forbid them not, for of such is the Kingdom of God." You and I have to return to the kid state, some part of us; not juvenile delinquency; but we have to get back to where the kid was and grow up all over again differently. This sourness and this bitterness and unenthusiasm for life—it can happen when you are 9, 19, 29, and doesn't have to happen when you are 100. It all depends. "In the beginning was the Word."

Now an idea which persists will take form. Someone said, "A man who seeks one thing in life, and *but one*, may hope to achieve it before life is done." Ideas are realities; but if that is true and our ideas are mixed, part happy and part unhappy, we will draw some happiness and some unhappiness. The law of attraction and repulsion works with mathematical invariableness, with absolute immutability, with exactness. Whatsoever a man thinks—that will happen to him. If it had to be *created* it would happen!

Therefore if we see part of the time that everything is good, part of the time it isn't, we suffer the dualism of good and evil. There is no such thing as good and evil in the Universe; there is no dualism or duality in it. *There is nothing but God.* But because of the creative power of our thought, even that which is good can appear to us as evil. One man's meat is another man's poison.

They criticized Jesus because they said he was evil. He didn't criticize them, because he knew everything is in a process of evolution. We belong to a philosophy which believes that there is nothing but God and that each one of us represents the Eternal. We sputter and spit and fuss around, throw brickbats at each other. I said to one of our leaders the other day, "Isn't it funny; all of us spend about half our time denying what we believe, sort of arguing with each other—not meanly—and the rest of the time we spend praying everything will come together good. If we split the difference, there wouldn't be much left, would there? That is the trouble with us: sometimes hot, sometimes cold." One of the poets said, "None of the singers ever yet has fully lived his minstrelsy"; and Jesus said, "If you want to know of this doctrine, try it." Love only knows and comprehendeth love. Who knows what might happen to an individual, a human, who knew nothing but love?

I tried a very interesting experiment recently when I was in Florida. (I didn't want to go—there were other things I wanted to do—but I had promised; so I went and spoke in four cities in Florida, where I am not known.) I thought to myself, What can I do for somebody whom I do not know? And we had big crowds everywhere I went; they all seemed so much like our own people. And I said, Well, I shall demonstrate to myself that I love these people. God is Love, and I love people anyway. It is only my business if love is transmitted. What is everything else? And I did it: every place I went, strangers came up to me and said, "It must be the most wonderful thing in the world to be loved by so many people!" Isn't that something?

"Who loses his life will find it." We have to surrender the opposite, the negation, if everything is made by the Word. And an idea shall prevail, persistently held—not like holding thoughts; not that way. Sort of good-natured flexibility. There is no dualism; Hell is cooled off; the Devil is dead. Someone will say, "You are a fool." But *who* gets fooled-?!

So they crucified Jesus. We say, "Oh, the agony of the cross, the betrayal!" What is three days in eternity? And no human being has ever been loved the way Jesus has been loved. He wasn't crucified at all—he had a few hours of exquisite triumph, that is all. And in the exaltation of that ecstasy, he said two things that flow across the pages of history like a beacon light—and should have destroyed what is false in every theology: "Father, forgive them, for they know not what they do." And to the thief, "Today shalt thou be with me in paradise."

So they killed Socrates, the father of philosophy—and as he was dying, he laughed because Plato was crying, and he said to his other followers, "Plato thinks that *this* is Socrates, that they will kill him; and I said, 'They will have to catch me first.' I shall stay where I am." He was never caught. What were the few moments of the trial?

117

Who is the man who changed the intellectual history of the human race?

So they shot Abraham Lincoln, the most beloved of all Americans. So Gandhi was killed; and the last thing he did was to make their sign of forgiveness. He knew. These have been the great and good and wise. No: we measure things with too small a measure; the infinite ocean is beside us, and we dip it up with a thimble.

Who is there among us who remains true to an idea for one hour, one day, one week, one month, one year, one life . . . ? I believe everything is made up out of thought. I believe there is nothing but the action and reaction of the Intelligence of the Universe, giving birth to all of Its laws, which work with mathematical certainty. That is right along the line with modern science: the infinite Thinker thinking mathematically. God is Love thinking lovingly; Goodness, Truth, and Beauty. I love beauty and cannot live without it. I would starve without it. Because there is more than physical starvation: there is esthetic starvation, there is starvation for lack of a thought of love.

Physical starvation is very simple; it only takes a few weeks. The other might go on for a lifetime—of fear, of the impoverishment and lack of living the creative life, till the joy has gone out of everything, everything sours, and we are no longer "jubilant and beholding souls, with nimble hands and running feet" to look up and laugh in the face of the Universe, and say, "Hello, God!" When that has gone out, we are temporarily dead. But never can we quite lose that Thing which is implanted—that Spark which we may desecrate but never quite lose. So we are living in the possibility of limitless abundance.

Now I happen to believe we are playing around with the most terrific idea the world has ever known. I believe Religious Science is the religion of the future. I don't think it is any of my business or yours—it is bigger than we are. I believe we ought to prove to the world that here is a group of people who demonstrate every step they take. I am taking definite steps in my own thought now to formulate some plan for the working out of that which I think will be better done throughout all our churches next year, because they all are tolerant enough to try what I suggest.

"These signs shall follow them that believe." Belief is an idea, a thought, an acceptance. But how can we both believe and not believe? Therefore we are confused. Everyone should be successful. I don't mean have a million dollars. I don't have much but have everything I need. I wouldn't want to just give my time to making money. If I didn't have it, I would give all my time to it. I think everybody should live well—*everybody*. We are just missing something. We *have* it, but we *miss* it. We hold it in our hand, but it falls away from us. We embrace it in our desire but do not embody it in our thoughts. We are a house divided against itself. We *ought* to be well, we *ought* to be prosperous, we *ought* to be happy. You and I, as we meet people—there should be a healing power emanating from us which will heal them without our even knowing it.

This is what we believe, this is what we must prove: *the power of acceptance.* Someone will say, "I don't know enough." *No one* knows enough. There isn't anyone living who knows how you can think or breathe or how your blood can circulate or how a bird can sing—there is no one living; and all the science and art and philosophy and wit and theology of man cannot tell you how a ham sandwich can become brains or blood or fingernails. They just don't know. All they can do is watch and tabulate the actions and reactions of an invisible guest or ghost or whatever it may be. That is all they know, all you know, all I know.

Therefore you and I know just as much—and more—about our science than any physicist. We know infinitely more about the human mind than all the psychologists put together, because all they studied is the abnormal mind—and about the *normal* mind they know very little if anything. I have the greatest respect for doctors and surgery and everything—but there isn't a surgeon in the world knows how your blood can circulate. He knows there are certain things have to happen that it may; if there are obstructions, it can't—and he tries to remove them. That is all any of us can do.

You and I know just as much about the Science of Mind as is known, in its field, about the science of electricity. Just exactly. Now stop ignorantly and stupidly denying your own capacity. *We must not do it.* Don't undersell yourself before the court of the Almighty. If God saw fit to make you and me, we *belong*, and we are *needed*, and God Himself would be incomplete without us—or He never would have made us. Now this calls for persistency of an idea: you can heal everybody you touch, you can bring joy and gladness and love and rationality to every environment, by just knowing you can—that silent invisible flow; "flow, sweet river, flow" —but we cannot do it until we first have admitted it and accepted it.

I want to see the time—and expect to see it—when

everyone who comes into one of our meetings who needs healing will go out well. It ought to be that way; it is wrong if it isn't that way. We haven't put the thing together right if we don't do it. We are not to be blamed; it isn't our fault: we just haven't done it. And we should not criticize ourselves for not having done it. All the wealth of the world cannot compensate for this. There is nothing the world can give us in exchange for the coin of the eternal Kingdom of the everlasting God. Jesus didn't need a baker: he could multiply the loaves and fishes; he didn't need a banker: he could find money in the fish's mouth. Why don't *we*?

We haven't quite remained true enough to an idea, merely because we didn't *know* or couldn't bring ourselves to *believe*. Maybe we are a little overmodest spiritually. Now we ought to be modest intellectually and physically and humanly. But spiritually we don't have to be modest. What God Almighty did must be pretty good. We don't have to be ashamed that we are alive. We are not worms of the dust or unworthy creatures to be snatched from the mouth of a burning abyss. That is all nonsense. We are not weaklings. "Who hath told thee that thou art naked?"

There isn't anybody going to tell me that I am outcast from the Kingdom of God; for when I look up and see the glory of Heaven and the beauty and warmth and color of the evening sunset, look across the horizon and see the golden glow of approaching day and the sun spilling its warmth through the chariots of fire across the hilltops to awaken the valley, nurture it, and bring joy to it—I don't think I am so unworthy. Maybe the physical, the intellectual is; maybe I'm stupid; but I believe I can reach down and find a grandeur there, a simplicity; and I do spend much time all alone in the middle of the night—any time, hours upon hours sometimes—and I can feel it, and I know it, and it is as real as this, and as solid; and it belongs to everybody.

And I thought last night, I better go to bed, because the time changes.* And I said, No; I want to sit here a while longer. I want to see what happens; I want to invite whatever this Thing is that made me, to flow through me. I want to open myself to It. This is the Lover of the soul —that part that makes whole, without which we are but a makeshift that camouflages or counterfeits. Just a tiny speck of that divine Possibility already incarnated within us.

You and I are the chosen people of the ages (because *we* choose *It*, *It* chooses *us* automatically), without fear, believing that we are worthy; but with true humility, as an artist feels humble before the beauty of things even in the "exaltation of his beholding soul." "O beauty," he feels, "engulf me; O warmth and color, flow through me." So Kipling said: when this happens, "No one shall work for money, and no one shall work for fame, / But each for the joy of the working, and each, in his separate star, / Shall draw the Thing as he sees It for the God of Things as They are."

That is the way it is. "Shouting and tumult cease, / The captains and kings depart. / Still stands thine ancient sacrifice / And humble and a contrite heart." Sure, we are humble before God, great beauty, the terrific impact of the Cosmos upon our soul. But we are proud without arrogance, we are exalted without conceit in the face of

*I.e. the clock would be advanced an hour for Daylight Saving Time.

men. We have a destiny to perform; we are here for a purpose, individually and collectively, to prove before the world that He has not left Himself without a witness.

This is a beginning. Yesterday is past, tomorrow is not here, today salvation presses itself against us. The Chinese sage said, "O man: having the power to live, why will ye die?" And Jesus said, "O Jerusalem, thou that stonest the prophets, how often would I have gathered thee together, even as a hen doth gather her chickens, but thou wouldst not."

God always would. Let us make up our minds that we are that chosen people—because *we* chose *It*. There shall no longer be evil in our sight; the eternal Good shall be alone without being lonely. The Infinite shall embrace us and God Himself go forth anew into His own Creation— because you and I believe; and looking up and seeing that which seems to deny our belief, we *still* believe. "Believest thou that I am able to do this?" "Yea, Lord, I believe." "Then be it done unto you as you believe." For all the world is made of belief; all the world awaits the dawn of a new spiritual renaissance. And everything in the Universe is hushed and the holy temple of the living Presence.

Dear God, we come. Amen.

AFFIRMATIVE-PRAYER MEDITATION

(We have this box with all the names, and every name is known to the One Mind, which is our mind too. Therefore we know and we answer and fulfill the needs of every person who has requested, whether it be healing or a betterment of life and circumstance. And with whoever asks for whatever good he or she needs we affirm the presence of that good, the elimination of everything that denies it. We identify this person with that good and know that this word going forth shall not return unto us or them void, but it does accomplish and it is accomplishing and we bless it and bless each here and now.)

Now may the eternal light of the living Spirit which is God—that silent, invisible, but ever-present Partner and Host whom we recognize—may this Living Presence be so real to us that It shall radiate, heal, and bless and help. Eternal Spirit within us, bring the joy of Your Presence, the love of your givingness, the abundance of your Wealth, the perfection of your Wholeness, and the joy of your Soul into our lives, that we shall sing and dance in the sunlight of eternal Truth, forevermore. Amen.

CHAPTER 8

How to Claim Your Freedom

Dr. Holmes in his early days had been a "Play Reader" in the northeastern part of the United States. In those days of the early 1900s, small communities looked forward to the appearance of a good "Play Reader." The Reader sat on a stage with nothing on it but his stool and a stand to hold the Reading. The Reader read with feeling all the parts of the play.

These early experiences stayed with Dr. Holmes all his life. He always objected to too much furniture and flowers or too many people on his lecture platform. Somehow when he spoke from a theater platform, he created a deep person-to-person bond with his audience. I was there with him many times and have selected some of his memorable talks at the Wiltern Theater. These have been released at one time or another since then in sterilized or predigested form—but we have them here just about verbatim.

I T IS A great privilege to be here and take Bill's* place while he and his family are having a vacation.

I have arranged my talks in a series of lessons: I am not an orator; I am a teacher. I have just spent part of the

---

*William H.D. Hornaday.

last two weeks lecturing in New York at the INTA* Congress. I was invited to speak in nearly every country in the world, and practically all the states. We really have the best and clearest metaphysical teaching on earth. There is no question about it in my mind.

There is no question in my mind but what we are the next greatest religion of the future—because the religion of the future will be a combination: it will come from science, from philosophy, and from religion. It will come as science becomes less and less materialistic, which it is now doing; when philosophy stops being dualistic, as though there were a material and a spiritual universe—or just a material; and when theology gets over its superstition. When I lost Hell, I lost the greatest asset I had: there is nowhere to send people who disagree with me; and that is bad. I miss it more than any of my infantile possessions; but I couldn't carry it along into adulthood —because the place cooled off long ago.

Now we bring together these great things; and I want to show you in the next three Sundays something I think it is very necessary for us to know: how to help yourself and others; how to prosper yourself and others; and how to make yourself and others happy. We believe in a practical religion. It has to be practical, something people can use.

I had the privilege of going last Sunday morning to hear Norman Vincent Peale.† His place is so crowded, but we called up Saturday and they very kindly reserved

*The International New Thought Alliance.
†Pastor of New York's Marble Collegiate Church and author of *The Power of Positive Thinking* and other books. Dr. Peale, on this as on numerous other occasions, acknowledged Dr. Holmes as having exerted a significant influence on his thought.

seats. His talk could have been given right here. It is just as metaphysical as any we give; and he truly is a great man and recognizes the principles we believe in and teaches them. Being still in the "Church," he is bound to be a little restricted. But he is less restricted than any man I have ever heard from the pulpit. Well, that isn't saying much, because it is the first time I've been to church in 25 years; so I don't know anything about it.

He is a very generous man. I went down front; he turned to a large group of people and said, "This is a man from whom I have gotten so much." Only a man who has arrived dares to say these things. Little people are so little that they hate even to lose their *littleness*—because it is all they have left. But a man like this, who encompasses a larger picture, isn't afraid to admit there is someone else in the world.

I want to talk this morning on How to Help Yourself and Others in Freedom—how to be free. What do we mean by being free? Being free does not mean doing just as we please, because no one can do just as he pleases and get away with it. The truth that makes us free, enabling us to claim our freedom, must of necessity be a truth that does not deny the Unity of Good. Our freedom cannot be at the expense of others. We do have a freedom to love and be loved; but a woman does not have the freedom to pick out some man, whether he is married or single, and treat that he will fall in love with her. And she had better not try it!

We have a freedom to express all there is, but no freedom to rob someone else. Not the slightest. I believe each one of us is an individualized God. That is quite a claim to make! We are individual infinites. I'll tell you why I think so; I don't want to believe anything just because it pleases me. That would be silly. We are really scientific, intelligent, philosophic, deep thinkers—but spontaneous human beings: we are not afraid of life. The greatest background I have had was that I was brought up in an atmosphere where fear was not known and superstition was not taught, but reverence and adoration and worshipfulness were generated. No meal was ever said without prayer; everyone prayed at night. But there was no fear. I was grown up before I knew people actually believed there was a devil and a hell and had a fear of God and the Universe in which they lived. It must be a terrible thing.

But we can be free of superstition and free of fear— but we must not be "free of ignorance": *we are thinkers.* Seneca* said, "Keep faith with reason, for she will convert thy soul." You and I are individualized centers in God. No two persons are like; no two thumbprints are alike; therefore I feel we will never be reproduced. That is why Emerson said, "Take yourself for better or for worse. Imitation is suicide." Now since God is One, there is only one God, only one of whatever It is. Life is one, since God is one. God is not cut in two, as though part of God were here and part of God were someplace else. All of God is everywhere, just as all the mathematics there is, all the harmony there is, all the abstract beauty there is, all the gravitational force that there is, is everywhere.

Gravitational force will hold a peanut on the piano or the Empire State Building in place—it doesn't know any-

*Lucius Annaeus Seneca (4 B.C.?–A.D. 65), Roman statesman, philosopher, and dramatist.

thing about big or little or hard or easy. You and I are surrounded by a Presence which is God the Spirit, and a Power which is God the Law, and these are the two great realities. The Presence we may talk to, and It will answer: there is a communion. The Power is like every other law in the Universe: It obeys, It follows, our word; It does unto us as we believe. And that is why affirmative prayer works. It is a statement: *there is a Power greater than we are, and we can use It consciously.*

But we could not use that Power to destroy that Power or to destroy God or ourselves. Therefore we can use that Power in Its greater sense only as we use It in love, in givingness, in peace, in joy, and only as we use It constructively. I believe all the Power there is in the Universe is delivered to each one of us for his individual use. Now that is quite a thing to say.

I was teaching a class in New York the other day, and I said, "We do not teach that we have power. We teach that Power *is*, and we use It. We do not say that this person is a natural healer, or is any kind of healer, or has a healing power, any more than we would say that this man has electricity or that he has mathematics. He doesn't *have* gravitational force; he is *in* it, and it operates upon him. He has the freedom in gravitational force to move about; we have the freedom in the Law of Good, which is creative, to be or do anything that belongs to the natural Law of the Universe, way beyond anything you and I could think of.

I believe the time will come when they will multiply the loaves and fishes scientifically. Jesus never did anything that can't be done, you know. He only did what *can* be done. What *can't* be done, never was done by anyone.

129

Even Jesus never broke the laws of the Universe. He understood how to comply with them.

He transported himself from place to place at will without using a conveyance. Doctor Rhine* at Duke University has scientifically demonstrated in the last 25 years that we can reproduce the activities of the five senses without using the organs of sense. Now that is something! He has proven we can think without using the brain. He has demonstrated that without using the physical body or brain we can exist and continue and be conscious. That is a scientific demonstration of immortality, right now. Job said, "In my flesh shall I see God." That is terrific—coming out of a psychological laboratory of a major university.

Now Jesus multiplied loaves and fishes, raised the dead and healed the sick, brought the boat immediately to the shore, did all kinds of things we call miracles. But there are no miracles in God's Life. God is the same yesterday, today, and tomorrow, and never departs from His own Being. Jesus understood something which he referred to as the truth that shall make us free. He said there is a Truth, and "the truth shall make you free."

Now that Truth would have to be something we *know* —not something we *do*. You and I cannot create the Truth. That thing which makes us free and happy and prosperous is something that everybody has but very few people use, because very few people believe in it. And even the ones who believe: very few of them use it scientifically, accurately, and with absolute certainty of result.

*J.B. Rhine (1895–1980), American psychologist, founder and director of the Institute of Parapsychology at Durham, N.C.

Now we want *results. We want them!* I *want* to see the time, and I *expect* to see the time, and I am *going* to see the time—because definite steps are being taken, and motion under my direction to prove—that everyone who comes into our audiences will be healed. I don't think it is any of their business: I don't think what they believe has anything to do with it. You might not believe you would get wet if you got in the water; but if you got in the water, you would be wet.

The laws of Nature are no respecter of persons. There is a Power greater than we are; there is a freedom beyond anything you and I have ever experienced. And the world is waiting for some person and some group of persons who, without superstition or saying, "Look at me and die," will have something that can be delivered to the sinner as well as the saint—because there is so little difference between a sinner and a saint that I always get them confused (and generally have more fun with the sinners).

I believe life is *Living*. I was at the convention* for eight days. I spoke lots of times but had time to see two of the best shows I have ever seen, go to three parties, to prayer meetings twice, and a banquet once. I think that is living it up. Life is not a continual prayer meeting. Like the little boy who told his grandmother that if she ever went to a circus, she would never go to a prayer meeting again.

As a matter of fact, a prayer meeting should be the most exciting thing we could go to. It should become the most exhilarating experience we could have. It should unleash all the creative ability and imagination we have,

---

*I.e. the INTA Annual Congress (1958).

because at a prayer meeting where people who believe get together, such a power ought to be loosed that an angel chorus would sing. There should be a light, like "the light that lighteth every man's path," that everyone would be aware of. There should be a sense of a deep and abiding peace and stillness. I said the other day something I have learned by experience: every person will be alone until he is not lonely. Every person will listen to the silence until it speaks. Every person will be compelled to look at darkness until he sees a light. And every man will lie in his own grave until he resurrects himself. And that is true.

You and I have the power; but what do we do with it? Surely a prayer meeting—right here, this, today—should be the most interesting thing that ever happened to you or to me! We should come to see today—with a dynamic, creative imagination and a deep inward feeling and conviction—that we have been playing around the edge of a stupendous Possibility. The ancient Chinese sage said, "O man, having the power to live, why will ye die?"

I thought yesterday (nine hours on a plane coming home; it is such a terrific thing to have breakfast in New York and supper at home at night), "Time is not, and space is not"—but experience is. And I thought: What are you telling these sweet people tomorrow who will take an hour out to come and listen to you? This little tiny ego: will you get your big feet out of the way? And I said, Probably not; because we have to maintain a good-natured flexibility, even with ourselves, to get along in life. I prayed several hours, and I thought: If just this much revelation of the Self to the self can come, then we will all be glad. I'll be glad because you cannot give without receiving; you'll be glad because you cannot receive without giving. Everything moves in a cycle or circle; and "With what measure ye mete, it shall be be measured to you again."

Now there is a Power greater than we are, and we can use it. It is creative—It can do anything—and It responds to our belief in It; but our belief in It has to be a belief that It is *now* operating and that It *has* operated. Someone will say this calls for faith. *All life* calls for faith. I thought the other day, if you and I had the same faith that an electrician has, we would be better metaphysicians. Religious people do not have the faith that scientists have. When scientists have demonstrated a principle, there is no longer any question in their mind.

There is a Power that responds to our consciousness exactly the way we think, like a mirror; and if I say— no matter what it looks like—"I am surrounded by love and by friendship; I *am* love, I *am* friendship; I give and I receive and I believe it, and this is true *now*," the machinery and the mechanism of the universal Law of Cause and Effect is set in motion to make it come true, and nothing can destroy it unless I do, myself; nothing can neutralize it. I know there are people who say, "Well, you have to have a great spiritual understanding." *I* haven't met them,* and I stopped looking for them 35 years ago. "There are no prophets other than the wise."

If a person comes to me now and says, "I have it all; I know it all." I say, "All right, go out there; there is a paralyzed man: tell him to get up and walk." In our business, you have to put up or shut up, and that is good enough for me. All the professions of faith make no

_____
*I.e. people with the "great spiritual understanding."

difference. Unless action follows, "methinks the lady doth protest too loudly," as Shakespeare said.

We follow a scientific—that is, a sure—method. We now know, as they have demonstrated down at the University in Redlands, that a prayer—we call it a treatment —is an affirmation of acceptance. Now why is it? Because you have to plant a seed before it can grow; that is all. Why does God make it so you have to plant the garden before you can get a garden? Just because that is the way it works. Why do you have to move a thing from place to place so gravity will hold it? Just because you have to.

Now there are certain things in the Universe that have to be accepted. We didn't make them; we can't change them. I don't think God made them—I think that is the way God is. Therefore it is said that God's language is "yea and amen."* We have to live an affirmative life, and that is that; and it isn't because God hates us or is trying to test us. All this theory that we are here to be tested to see if we are worthy to endure is just so much nonsense. We are here for the delight of whatever It was that created us—just as our whole life exists for the expression of our soul. What else could it be for? Life is made to live, a song is made to sing, and a dance to dance. We have to be glad; we have to be happy.

Now we have a *freedom* for all these things that belong to the nature of God. We have freedom to love. What is to stop me from loving you? Nothing but myself. It wouldn't be any of my business whether you loved me; but if I loved you enough, you would. What is to stop me from being glad? It won't hurt anybody. It won't save

*2 Cor. 1:20.

anybody for me to be sad. Jesus said, "And I, if I be lifted up"—not dragged down—"will draw all men to me." There is nothing to keep me from being glad. Nothing. What is to keep me from having peace of mind? Some-one says, "There is so much confusion in the world that I can't have peace of mind." There has *always* been con-fusion in the world, and there *will* be in the world as long as I live; therefore shall I be confused? *No!* I want peace of mind. I can't live without it.

I had to go away the last two weeks every day some-times for a couple of hours to do what I call "putting myself back into myself." I met so many people and talked to so many people.* I have to have equilibrium and joy and peace of mind and balance and poise inside of me or else I get dragged apart, or something. I don't know what happens, but it isn't good. It isn't good for anybody either; you can shatter anything. Walt Whitman said he liked to take time to loaf and invite his soul, and we all ought to take time to loaf and invite our soul.

Here is the cause of all creation; here in you and in me is the possibility of all joy; here is the freedom we have been looking for—and we shall never find it outside. Never. Therefore if I love enough, I shall be loved. I never experienced so much love in my life as I have in the last two weeks—but I went prepared for it. I treated myself to know I loved everyone I would meet; and so many people said to me, "Isn't it wonderful to be loved the way you are?" And I said, "Well, I love people, that is all."

Love and you shall be loved. But we separate two or three people and say we love *them*; or love must come to

*I.e. at the INTA Congress.

us from this or that person. This is not love we are after. Nothing wrong about it; but there is nothing can keep me from loving everyone. Nothing. I have this freedom. Do I have an equal freedom to hate everyone? *No.* I'll tell you why. Emerson said, "Nature forevermore screens herself from the profane."

Menninger* wrote a book called *Love Against Hate*: love is a principle in nature; hate is chaos. We can hate until it poisons us, destroys the liver, creates inaction, and kills us. Then we may get a fresh start, and that is all that death is—not to the soul, which lives forever. Browning said a man may desecrate that part, but he cannot lose it. So you see, I do not have an *equal freedom* to hate; I have the *possibility* of hating for a short time.

The more I hate, the worse I'll be; the more I love, the better I'll be: that is my freedom. That is why Tolstoy said we have freedom within the laws of inevitability, by which he meant we have freedom to be lined up with the laws of God. But how could we have freedom to destroy this Universe? The great fallacy of communism, fundamentally, is that in the name of liberty it is destroying freedom, and in the name of unity it is trying to create uniformity. [Robotization and uniformity:] neither one of these things exists in nature. That is why it cannot stand. The trouble isn't economic or political—that is bad enough for us; we wouldn't like it—but fundamentally it is denying two of the great propositions in the universe: [first, that there is freedom, not robotization; second,] that there is unity but not uniformity—that all nature tends to individualize everything, and the common denominator is in Spirit and not in a monotonous repeti-

*Karl Menninger, American psychiatrist.

tion of likeness (which is a great fallacy). Fundamentally, that is why it cannot exist beyond a certain time—I don't know how long; but it can't.*

We have the freedom to be happy. Now why aren't we? A few people we permit to rob us of our happiness. We say, unless love comes through them, we won't get it. Then we are always projecting our inadequacy or morbidity, fear. And every time they think of us, they don't like us—because they can't; because they are getting the vibration of our relationship.

Everything works with mathematical accuracy. Love everybody. Be glad. "There is ever a song somewhere, my dear." Let's sing it. We have the freedom to be happy; we have the freedom to be at peace, to be poised, to be calm. Now we all "know" these things. Everybody says, "Well, I follow you; I believe in what you say; that is right; *but look at all the other things!*"

Do we have a freedom to be well? Do we have a freedom to be prosperous? I think we do. I think freedom includes all these things. It is now known that the vast majority of disease—way above 75 percent—is emotional in its nature. That doesn't mean it is unreal. It's silly, to me, for people to say that sickness isn't sickness—of course it is; or poverty isn't poverty—of course it is. But that doesn't mean it *has* to be. I believe we have the freedom to be happy, to be well, and to be prosperous. Why shouldn't we, in a Universe the nature of which is so extravagantly abundant and so abundantly extravagant?

We have the freedom to be happy. I don't think there

*The reference, again, is to communism. Dr. Holmes' words proved to be prophetic long before most were prepared to accept their validity. See also *Holmes Papers*, vol. 2, pp. 50, 51.

is anything worthwhile without happiness. If a person isn't happy, what is worthwhile? We *ought* to be happy. But how are we going to be well, happy, prosperous unless we believe in some fundamental things that we can prove, and prove them right here and now—not in the by-and-by, not when we have shucked off this mortal coil. *Right now.* Whatever is true, is true *now.* *This* is the time; *we* are the people; *this* is the day; *you and I* are the ones; *here* is the place. *Right now.*

We have to make up our mind, and it isn't going to be easy always. Emerson said it is easy enough in solitude to do all these things; but, he said, the great man is he who in the midst of the crowd shall keep with perfect simplicity the independence of his solitude. How true that is! We don't want to retire from life or go away from living; we want to live right here where it is. It isn't so bad. It is pretty good, I think. *People* are pretty good too. Love is the thing that reveals the goodness of people—the kindness, compassion, tenderness, sympathy. We are a little afraid of it. I think the greatest ovation I ever received in my life was night before last, and I didn't speak over seven minutes; but it ended on the right kind of a note — of beauty, of sympathy, of love, of unity, and of togetherness. And then I said: "I love you all." I have never received such an ovation in my life.

Now New York people are like Los Angeles people. We are all alike. People respond. Aren't we just a little bit afraid of it? Some big, strong man thinks he wouldn't want to be sentimental. Some sweet woman thinks she wouldn't want to be misunderstood. To be misunderstood is not bad. I have been misunderstood all my life, and I hope I always shall be—because I would like to keep a little ahead always of this humdrum, monotonous, silly sense that people have. Emerson said, "Over the doorway of consistency I would write, Thou Fool."

We want to be spontaneous, we want to have joy, we want to have love, we want to have prosperity, we want to have health. These are things I want to discuss with you in the next few weeks. We *can* have them; they belong to us; but "Each, in his separate star, / Shall draw the Thing as he sees It / For the God of Things as They are." You don't have to go outside yourself to demonstrate all these things. Your prayer is just as good as mine: it is God that makes the prayer and God that answers it. That is why it can't be a petition. It is an affirmation. And that is why Emerson said, "Prayer is the proclamation of a jubilant and a beholding soul."

Let's see during this next week before we come together to discuss how to do all these things (next Sunday morning in our first great lesson)—let's train our minds this week to be affirmative. Let's get up in the morning and say, "I am going to live and I am going to be happy today. I am going to receive joy and life and love and laughter from everyone, and I am going to give them to everyone; and everyone shall be divine to me. This is the day that God has made, and I shall be glad in it." And let us give thanks every night and know that we shall sleep in peace and wake in joy and live in a consciousness of Good.

Let's see if you and I this week cannot get just a little bit better acquainted with the Guy inside of us. He is wonderful. He is terrific. He has talked to me so much these last three weeks, more than ever in my life—up in the Adirondacks and down in that teeming city. This is no stranger. This is no alien. Speak to Him, then, for He hears; and "spirit with Spirit shall meet; / Closer is He than breathing, / Nearer than hands and feet." I don't care if somebody thinks I am over-religious or sentimental. I am so religious that it *doesn't* hurt! I am so religious that it *helps*! But I wouldn't give a nickel for all the theology that was ever written.

Who told all these guys what is the possibility of my soul? Who shall tell me when that divine moment comes? Emerson said, "Leave all of your theories as Joseph left his coat in the hands of the harlot, and flee. To you alone shall come the wonder and the majesty and the power and the might and the exquisite sweetness of communion with the Ineffable, the beauty of the divine Presence, the glory of the eternal Light, and the peace of your own soul."

AFFIRMATIVE-PRAYER MEDITATION

(We have lots of people who have asked for help, and let's start right out with the belief that we *can* help them; and after we have treated them, I would like to spend a few minutes doing what I call "stretching the mind." The intellect may analyze, dissect, accept, or reject; but there is an intuitional faculty back of the intellect that knows more than the intellect. We do not all grab it right up like that. Therefore we have to train the intellect to reach a place where it receives this greater illumination. And that is what I mean by stretching the mind.

(I'll show you exactly what I mean. If it doesn't seem like much to you, forget it—it won't hurt my feelings; but it seems terrific to me. It is merely a practice of identifying ourselves with a larger life. This was the genius of Walt Whitman; it is what is called by Bucke* "illumination of cosmic consciousness": the intellect identifies itself with the Spirit until it makes possible a greater influx of the Spirit into the intellect.

(But first of all, let us know that everyone who has asked for help, whose name appears here in this box, now does receive that for which he has asked. And if he is here in this room, as he probably is, let him or her know that right now we are affirming the presence of the good desired. We are denying any substantial reality to that which does not belong. We are establishing him in our own consciousness in the Kingdom of God, which is an ever-present Reality here and now. As we sit here, we expect everything that does not belong to dissolve as mist before the light of the sun, as snow would melt in the heat of the sun.)

There is one Life, that Life is God, that Life is his life or her life—each one who has made a request; and as we sit here, that Life, that Light, is manifesting Itself. And how wonderful it is to know that we do affirm It, we do accept It without effort; and we do rejoice that it is so—as it must be.

*Richard M. Bucke (1837–1902), Canadian psychoanalyst and author of *Cosmic Consciousness*.

Silently the miracle of life transpires, silently this Good takes form, and we accept it.

(And now for a few moments let us practice together what I call "stretching the mind." Maybe you have never done it or thought of it, but it doesn't matter. It is a process whereby one identifies himself with a larger good after this fashion—he speaks in the first person pretty much:)

There is one Life, that Life is God, that Life is my life now. "I am that which Thou art, Thou art that which I am." I am one with all the beauty of life; I am one with the strength of the wind and the wave, the glory of the sunset, the beauty of the sunrise. I am one with the song of the birds; I am one with the mother holding her child; I am one with the babe drinking from the fountain of life. I am that which Thou art, eternal Spirit forever blessed; Thou art that which I am, perfect Presence, divine expanding within me. I am one with the vast throng in the busy street, one with the silence and solitude of Nature and the strength of the mountain and the peace of the desert. I am one with the rain and the snow and the clouds in the sky, the life in the ocean. I am one with the lover, one with the beloved. All are encompassed within me—for now what we are doing is identifying ourselves with the eternal living Presence within which all things are. We are one with That; That is what we are. "I am that which Thou art, Thou art that which I am," eternal Presence forever blessed, eternal Peace within me. "O living

Truth that shall endure when all that seems shall suffer shock"—"Before Abraham was, I am"—forever I shall be, encompassing planets and universes and time and space and the heart of God. I am that which Thou art, O living Presence; Thou art that which I am—eternal in the now, in the here, and in this moment. It is so.

Now may the light of the eternal God be with us. May that light go before us, surround us, penetrate us. May the love of God and of each other encompass and enfold us, and eternal peace abide with us forevermore.

CHAPTER 9

How to Help Yourself and Others

I T IS A great joy to be here this morning in Bill Hornaday's place while he is taking a vacation and much
deserved rest. I want to express my appreciation for this
magnificent audience. It is really terrific to have an audience like this in the middle of the summer, and very
flattering. If my head turned easily, my neck would be
broken right now—and I certainly appreciate it. I worked
last night for an hour and again this morning treating just
to know I would say something that would compensate
you for coming. It would be terrible to come in here and
hear nothing, wouldn't it? Something that we can take
home with us: I know that *I* shall greatly benefit, and I
want *you* to.

We find we are in the midst of a building campaign,*
and I know you have been down and seen part of the
building. It seems slow, but it takes a long time; and Paul
Williams, our architect, tells me it is going to be the most
beautiful building on the Pacific Coast. It is going to have
the finest organ this side of the Salt Lake Tabernacle
organ. You all want to take part in it, and we all want

*For Founder's Church of Religious Science, Los Angeles.

you to; and there are pledge cards, or you can call me up or someone. Let's all give all we can to this building fund —it is a great privilege. We are forerunners in a campaign of spiritual freedom, intellectual integrity, and emotional stability in a spiritual world.

It is our privilege to take part in a new spiritual renaissance—I wouldn't be here if I didn't believe it—and to do something for future ages. All of you who have given your pledges, please be sure they are kept up in payment, and add to them; and you others make new ones; and let's see what we can do during this month. We want another $125,000; we have $275,000. Our goal is $400,000. Let's raise it to that this month, so when Bill comes back he will be even gladder than he was when he left.

Also, your pledge gifts can be mailed to Church Headquarters. So please look at our building down there and realize what a terrific thing we are doing for the world. And remember this: our whole endeavor rests on demonstration. We have no other authority. We ask for none other. That is why I am talking on How to Prosper Yourself and Others next week, How to Make Yourself and Others Happy the following week, and How to Help Yourself and Others today. Our work rests on demonstration. We have to put up or shut up. And those are difficult things to do. Somebody said three things have to be done in making a speech: stand up, speak up, and shut up. The last is probably the most important. We have heard lots of people who stood up and spoke up but forgot to shut up. Well, I have to shut up at exactly 15 minutes past 11. I have no choice. Otherwise, I would probably talk till 12.

Religious Science is a new thing in the world because it is not dogmatic. We have people who believe in reincarnation and people who do not believe in it. We have every sort and condition of spiritual endeavor here. We are a melting pot, in a sense, for people who are seeking a new spiritual freedom without losing the old values. We are the greatest experiment in spiritual life of modern times. A man whose name I won't mention—he is wealthy, well known, connected with the University of Southern California for many, many years—told me he considered we are conducting the greatest spiritual experiment since the dawn of Christianity. Now this man is considered one of the most intelligent, highly respected men in the educational life of the United States, head of a great institution.

Now I believe that is true. Why? Because we are not dogmatic. I am not a prophet. We haven't any saints. I don't know about Reg and George.* "Saint Reginald" and "Saint George" would sound all right; but "Saint Ernie" would sound awful—and if they ever do that to me, I'll haunt them if I'm dead, and have them arrested if I am living. "Saint Ernie" would be awful. "Saint George" might not be so bad—he is the one who slew the dragon. There has been a dragon in every spiritual culture and it stands for that which binds us to duality.

Religious Science hasn't very many dogmas: *it believes in God*. You will find, out in front, on a slip—if you haven't got it—*What We Believe*. I wrote it 30 years ago, and I want you to read it and study it and think about it. It is what you and I believe in, I guess. God is all there

*Reginald Armor and George Bendall, close associates of Dr. Holmes.

is; there isn't anything else. God is the dancer, the singer; there is one Singer, one Dancer, one Writer, one Mind—but each one of us individualizes all of God. It is a terrific but simple concept. The only God you will ever know you will discover within yourself. That doesn't mean that you are God. God is what I am, but *I* am not God, thank God!

But what *am* I made of *but* God? He is over all, in all, and through all. Now there are two fundamental things you and I believe, as I understand it. God is a divine Presence inhabiting eternity, and indwelling our own heart. I love that thought. The other day, I put my arms around somebody of whom I am very fond, and I said, "I think a lot of you." And then I said to myself quietly, "This symbolizes to me that my arms are around the world, around everyone I know and everyone I meet, whether I know him or not." Wouldn't that be the meaning of "underneath are the everlasting arms," beneath are the girders of the Almighty—?

There is something about you and me that is cosmic, universal, stretches over time and space; let us learn to think better of ourselves. You know, you don't have to be conceited or get a big head to say, "God made me, and God cannot make mistakes. No matter what it looks like, God did not make a mistake when He made me." *He didn't.* God cannot err. The Universe is never defamed. The laws of God cannot be broken.

Now Jesus understood this. The great claim that his soul made on God was that "God is what I am, where I am, as I am, right here and right now—behold, the Kingdom of God is at hand. There is one Life, that Life is God, that Life is my life now—perfect, complete." You and I believe in it. There is no evil entity in the Universe. We all experience evil and negation, but there is no entity of evil. The more we can turn to the Good, the less evil will be apparent or real in our experience.

God is a divine Presence in our heart, enabling us to think and know and will and do and recognize each other in God, to behold in each other the living Presence. How wonderful to look upon humanity and say, "I behold in thee the image of Him who died on the tree." It is wonderful. Love is the lodestone of life. Love is the only emotional security that is known to the mind of man. Love is the basis of everything, the divine Givingness. There is no security without it.

We believe we are surrounded by Love. Now we also believe we are surrounded by a Law—this is the next important thing—of Mind in action: something that acts creatively upon our thinking, always tending to produce it in form and project it in our experience the way we think it; "As a man thinketh in his heart, so is he." These are the two great pillars of our conviction. They have been believed in since time immemorial. The Law and the Love, the Presence and the Power. These are the tools we work with to help ourselves and others.

Now this means, in the simplest form, that you and I have the Power within us now—right now, right this morning, right here, just as we are. We haven't got to get converted, we haven't got to confess our sins. We haven't time for that. We haven't got to get somebody to save us; because if we are lost, nobody would know where to look for us. That would be a waste of time. You are your only saviour. Jesus knew this. "Why callest thou me good? There is none good save one." "It is expedient that I go away."

Now you and I have to wake up to the fact that the true Saviour, the true Redeemer, the Thing that all the great have told about—*we are.* "I am that which I am." We will never find salvation outside ourselves. You know it as well as I do. If you and I didn't know it, we wouldn't be here; we would be somewhere where they think that they can hitch their wagon to a star and be wafted off to the Elysian fields without any cooperation with the laws of their being. That cannot be. Fortunately, the Law of our own life is resident within us, arbiters of our own fate: freedom without licence.

We are surrounded by an intelligent creative Principle which operates upon our thought. Now that is the reason why some prayers are answered and some are not. Every prayer is answered in such degree as it accepts its own answer, and that is why down here at Redlands University they have discovered that the affirmative prayer is the only prayer that makes any material difference—70 percent above the others. Well, we will accept that. It is why Jesus said, "When ye pray, believe that ye have."

Now we are bringing this stuff right down to something we can consciously practice and use to help ourselves and others. You can do it just as well as I can. Anyone can do it. We are surrounded by a creative Intelligence that operates upon our thought, always acting to bring into our experience that which is like our thinking. We can what we call *treat.* Now what do we mean by *treat*? We mean that we think something, say something, articulate something affirmatively by accepting that it is now accomplished, and identify what we say with ourselves or with some person, place, or thing.

Now let's analyze that a little, because this is a lesson. What we want to do is be taught. There is no use being taught unless *we* do it. A Chinese sage said, "O man, having the power to live, why will ye die?" I said to George Bendall this morning at breakfast, "If I take this salt shaker and move it over here, I have changed its position in gravitational force. I pick it up again and put it over there. But *I* don't make it stay down here; *I* don't make it stay down there. I lift it from here and put it there, and it is acted upon by a force." He said, "Of course."

I said, "George, how many people does it take to lift the thing over and put it down and convince gravitational force that it will hold it in place?" He said, "Just one." I said, "All right. How many people does it take to have a prayer answered, an affirmation accepted, or to make a treatment effective?" He said, "Just one." "Well, I said, that is one of the things I want to tell this wonderful audience this morning: one with God is a majority." I thought last night, when I was treating for this occasion—because I believe in treating for everything; I know it works—I thought to myself, I want a few simple things to more completely convince myself: how many people does it take to plant a rosebush so that the law of growth and productivity and creativity will make it bloom? Just one. One with God is a majority.

Now we are going to have to know this; because otherwise we will always be looking for saints and saviours "over there," and we shall rush from one to another. Someone back East said to me there was a very wonderful man doing some wonderful things, and he was going to be here and there; and I said, "Now this is grand, this is perfect; but he can only reveal you to yourself. If you have to rush today from one kind of a saviour to another, and tomorrow to another one, looking wild-eyed—you are not going to get anywhere."

Get still; get quiet; still the turmoil of the outer sense. Be still and *know*: YOU are the one you have been looking for. You are going to have to do it before you can make a good treatment. Why? Because we either affirm or deny. We either believe in our own word or else we don't. Who can make us believe in our own word? Nobody but ourselves.

Now another thing I wanted to be sure and mention to you: a treatment must be independent of the person who gives it. Now this is important. When I go out and plant a garden, I walk away and leave it, and I know something is going to make it grow. Its growth—the law of its being, that which is going to react to it out of the Universe now —is independent even of myself, though I planted it. I was the gardener only. We speak of "making" a garden. We *plant* one. *Nature* makes the garden; "God gives the increase."

Now this is necessary to know, because we get so all tied up and get our great big feet and our little egos in the way and think we have to do so much. Let me tell you: the person who uses this Principle the most effectively is the one who is the most deeply inwardly convinced of a simplicity and an integrity of the Universe, and that he is the one who can do it. No conceit about it: he can *plant* the garden; the garden is independent of him. All right.

He can plant it for someone else. He can go over in the other guy's yard and plant the seeds if he has asked him to; he has identified the creativity with that man's garden. That is all the difference there is between helping yourself and others.

Now we would like to do this. Every man wants to help himself. We believe he ought to be well, happy, prosperous. We have no superstition about it. We believe anything that will help him is good, whether it is a pill or a prayer. We are not confused about that. All instrumentalities belong to God. The Gita says, "All paths of worship lead to Me—all shrines to Me alone belong." Don't be confused.

Now another thing. People say, "I am not good enough." I have lived a long, long time, yet I feel younger than I did 40 years ago because then I thought I was pretty responsible for everything and now I know I am not. It is a great relief to be able to set the Universe down and let it roll. It is a terrific thing. Takes a long time to learn it, too. I haven't found anybody who is "good enough" yet, and as long as a quarter of a century ago I stopped looking for them, because most of the ones who thought they were good were so uninteresting to me (I wouldn't say *stupid*).

You are plenty good enough, because God made you. What you have to ask yourself is not "Am I good enough?" Rather, "Is my thinking constructive enough? Do I love enough? Do I give enough? Am I happy enough? Am I kind enough?" These are the evaluations that are spiritual—not if you are "good enough." Of course you are good enough; and if anybody ever tells

you that you are not, remember this: he is but projecting his own unconscious sense of guilt onto you and
trying to hang it on your ears. Don't take it. Feel sorry
for him. Shakespeare said, "Methinks the lady doth protest too loudly."

So you are good enough. Then you are *spiritual
enough.* I don't know how spiritual "spiritual" is. How
more spiritual can you be than to believe that God is all
there is and to love and adore God and talk to God and
know you live in God and God lives in you—? I don't
think you have to worry about that. God is all there is.
You can't change it, and I didn't make it; we can only
accept it. It is a simplicity. *God is all there is.*

Then "Do I know enough?" This is a bad one. "Must
I take another class to get that sacred Lost Word?" Nonsense! There isn't enough in all that to even make a decent
dish of pea soup. *Of course* you know enough. If you
know how to think, you know enough. If you know how
to believe there is something greater than you are, you
know enough. The whole question is: do you *do* it?—and
do you *believe now* that your word is in prayer or in the
Law of Mind in action or is a seed of thought planted in
the Absolute and that it must bear fruit? The only difference between Jesus and others was that he said, "Heaven
and earth will pass away, but my word shall not."

Now remember this: *you* are the person; *this* is the
place; *now* is the occasion; *right here* is the time; the word
is in *your own mouth*; you are *good enough*; you *know
enough*; you are *spiritual enough.*

The next thought is: *"How* do I do it?" Not by concentration. I am not criticizing concentration—I don't

153

know anything about it. I do know it is wonderful. Where does a mathematician concentrate the law of mathematics? He doesn't. He *uses* it. Forget concentration. When you plant a seed you do not concentrate any creativity. You plant a seed!

Do you "hold thoughts"? Of course not. You let go of them. Do you *will* anything to happen? If you and I and all of us willed—until we dropped dead from exhaustion —that the world would be flat, it wouldn't flatten out a thing but our own heads. *Nothing*. We have to comply with the laws of Nature. Every scientist does; and we are scientists when it comes to using this Law.

All you do is to affirm and believe in your own affirmation. What do you convince? is next. Now remember these steps—they are very important: You *affirm* it; and the next thing is, after doing that, you must *let go* of it, kind of forget it—even though you return again to it the same day or the next day; but drop it. Now this, perhaps, is the most difficult of all things. This is where we have to have faith. But we are not having faith in a forlorn hope, but in a Law of Cause of Effect that we know exists. Here is where self-training comes in.

I said to myself the other day—because something didn't happen that I thought ought to happen, and at first I was disappointed—"Now look here, little guy!" ("Why so hot, little sir?" Emerson said.) "You just forget it! If that was the way for it to happen—it will!" Do not for one moment permit yourself to doubt what you are doing: *faith is acceptance, in the assurance of a Law that is now proven to exist*—and it *will* work. "I will work, saith the Lord, and who shall hinder me?"

You and I have that faith, but we use it negatively. We don't say that we have to think up an affirmation; every time you speak, you affirm, even though it be negatively. We must believe that *this is it*, and that it is going to work. Now every scientist has to have this kind of faith; he has learned that this thing works; and if you and I knew—just as we know that if we plant a garden it will grow, that when we plant a seed, it will "take"—we would have faith. And that is the way it works.

Next we must identify our word. Now that is simple enough: I write a letter and address it to somebody and send it to them—to their name and street number, city, state, and country—and then I throw it in the mailbox. I don't give it a thought. When you give a treatment, you say, "Now this is for myself," or think, "This is for myself"; or if it is for somebody else, you merely speak his name, or think it, and say, "This is for him [or her]." Now that is what I mean by identifying your treatment with some person, place, or thing.

If it is for some situation that needs harmonizing, you say, "This word is for this situation in this home [or this office]. There is harmony, there is unity, there is love, there is cooperation. This word removes every sense of confusion and doubt, uncertainty, antagonism, resistance, or resentment [whatever has to be eliminated]." You put it in the form of your own words and announce that it isn't there. This sounds funny, because it *is* there; but you take a little piece of ice and hold it in the heat of your hand, and it will melt, become liquid: there are no opposites to God—there is only one Power in the Universe, and in such degree as it is used constructively, it will take precedence over everything else. Where is the darkness when the light shines? "And the light shineth in darkness; and the darkness comprehended it not." That is, it had no power.

You are the person; *here* is the place; *today* is the time; *this* is the moment; the word is in *your own mouth*. It is an affirmative word. You speak it and believe it and identify it with what you want to happen and then let go of it, no matter who you are working for.

Now the next thing I would like very much to make plain—very much: do not, please, wait till you know more, get more spiritual, get a bigger understanding—and feel more weak in the stomach! *Please do not wait.* The garden that isn't planted won't grow; the seed that is not sown will not flourish. The word that is not spoken cannot act; the prayer that is not said and accepted cannot be answered.

Next, experiment with it. I think this is one of the most important things—to experiment with what you know. Take two or three people and work for them every day as well as yourself. You can't hurt anybody; and it will help you. Take time to affirm whatever you think, and don't be afraid to deny what appears—it has an eraser; it rubs it out like rubbing wrong numbers off a blackboard—and affirm for this person everything until you sort of relax and say, "Isn't it wonderful! This is the truth about him. There is peace and harmony and joy. There is success and everything that belongs—'all this and heaven too.' This word is for him and for myself and my family"; and build up a case remembering this.

I would like to put it this way: it is as though a universal Ear were listening to what you say and reacting upon it according to the realization of the logic. Now I want to make this plain. There is a universal Intelligence that reacts to our word creatively—there isn't any doubt about it—and it is all-powerful. God the Spirit is more than that, but this is God the Law. It is what you are using; this is the Principle of the Science of Mind and of every other metaphysical movement no matter what it calls itself. It has to be that way.

Therefore your argument, if you have one, is within yourself to convince yourself. Sometimes you will find yourself saying, "Now the truth about this person is that there is perfect circulation, perfect assimilation, and perfect elimination. There is no stagnation." You will make that flat denial. Why? To straighten out your own mind. But the Principle back of it is—and listen to this—*a mental and spiritual argument logically presented to mind.* This is the method that has healed and helped 90 percent of all people who were ever helped in the last hundred years by all the movements. They all use it, remember. An argument which contains more affirmation and denial, logically presented to mind, will produce a result which is resident in the conclusion of the argument. Is that clear? It is so terrifically important; but *the argument takes place in your own mind.*

This is a lesson on how to give a treatment, you know, and *you* are the fellow who is going to do it. You are going to do it this week. Now if you do this, you are going to get a great wallop out of it—and I am not afraid to use the word *wallop* in spiritual things: we don't have to sit around and look sweet and sad and anemic in order to believe in God. That is terrible. I like sort of a lusty, husky faith in the Infinite. Whoever told us we had to become emaciated to worship? Nonsense! Riley* said, "As it is given me to perceive, / I most certainly believe / That when a man's glad, plumb through, / God's pleased with him, same as you."

There is a laughter of God—let's laugh it. There is a song of the Universe—let's sing it. There is a hymn of praise—let's praise it. There is a joy, a beauty; there is a deep, abiding peace; let's experience it. Right now, today. If you believe what I say—you are a good practitioner. If you use it, you will produce splendid results—and that is the next thing: to prove it to yourself; and after perhaps long years of waiting, coming back to the only Center there is, a God of Heaven and earth—YOU—YOU— simple *you*, simple *me*; unimportant, apparently without much influence in the world—it doesn't matter—but in the integrity of our own souls, in the communion of our own spirit, in the exaltation of our own consciousness, we may yet prove to the world that God is in His Heaven, *now*.

You are that Heaven. What a wonderful experience! What great joy should accompany everything that we do—an expectancy, love. Love everything, praise everything, recognize all things, believe all things, accept all things; and "To thine own self be true, and it shall follow as the night the day, thou canst not then be false to any man."

*James Whitcomb Riley (1849–1916), American poet.

AFFIRMATIVE-PRAYER MEDITATION

(Now we have time for a treatment. We have in this box the names of those who have asked for help. Next Sunday I would like to talk to you on How to Prosper Yourself and Others. There *is* such a law. It is not telling you how to make money or get rich—I don't know or care anything about that; but there is a Law that will bring to us everything that makes life worthwhile and happy and prosperous—if we want to use it. It is very simple; we can understand it. It *will* work. And may I thank you for your great kindness. I know we are every day thinking love for Bill Hornaday during his vacation and knowing that every good thing is coming to him and to his wonderful family. We love and appreciate him very much.)

Now let us turn within and treat ourselves first, recognizing that we are divine centers in the Mind of God. Here within us is the living Presence. Here within us is the perfect Peace, the eternal Joy, the everlasting Good, the all-conquering Love—and we have absolute faith in it, and we know our word is the Presence and the Power and the Activity of the Living Spirit; and we know that every person in this room and every person who has made a request in this chest belongs to God, lives in perfection. Whatever doesn't belong to him is eliminated; whatever is true is revealed. The divine and perfect Pattern of his own being is manifest silently, simply—simply,

159

but with certainty. Everything that doesn't belong to God's good Man *is* eliminated—and we know it and he knows it; and we expect it and accept the authority of this word in joy. Everything that he does will prosper, because of all the power there is—Love, the living Spirit Almighty. Every request is accepted and manifest now.

Now as we turn to That deep within our own soul and mind and consciousness, registering each in his own name—the Name of the beloved Son of the eternal God, the Presence and Power of the Infinite, the Will of Good, the Givingness of Spirit, the Peace and that Light that lighteth every man's path—we accept the glory of the Kingdom of Good, now and forever and forever. It is so.

And now, living Spirit; and now, divine Intelligence and Light that lighteth every man's path: we go forth in joy to greet the eternal dawn, the everlasting radiance of the countenance of the living Spirit. And the love of God goes with us and ". . . makes its store / To a soul that was starving / . . . in darkness before." So shall our light and love envelop every person we meet and sing a song, a hymn. And God bless us and keep us forever.

CHAPTER 10

How to Make Yourself and Others Happy

I WOULD LIKE to talk about our Church and the new building. We are building the first Christian church that is absolutely free from dogma and superstition, that has a very high intellectual level but does not overlook the spiritual and the level of feeling. I would laugh myself to death if I thought *I* had anything to do with it. These things happen, and they are bigger than you and myself. It is happening to us. We are the forerunners of a new aspect.

We are a Christian denomination. Someone said we didn't believe in Jesus; of course we believe in Jesus—and we believe in Buddha too; we believe in Socrates; we believe in Abraham Lincoln! And more than everything else, we believe in our own soul—the only immediate testimony you and I will ever have that we exist or that God exists or that Jesus showed us a way. We believe in every Wayshower.

We are the first Christian denomination to be free from superstition, dualism, and dogma. We are taking part in building an international monument to Truth*—that is

*This probably refers to the construction of Founder's Church of Religious Science in Los Angeles.

all you have to say to anyone. So let us support that, and let us do it with love and great joy.

You know, Religious Science is not something I invented. I didn't make it up. I put a few flourishes to it—but it is the outcome of the thought and the feeling of the Ages and the great minds of many denominations and religions. It embraces all of them—Buddhism, Mohammedanism, Hinduism, Zoroastrianism, Taoism, Confucianism, Judaism, and all of the different sects of the Christian faith, of which there are about 250 in America, just as there are several hundred, in India, of the Hindus. It embraces the affirmative part of all of them and comes up with the idea that the Universe is chock full of God; "In Him we live and move and have our being." Each one of us is an outlet to God and an inlet to God. As Emerson said, you are dear to the Heart of the Universe, and if God hadn't had need of you, He would not have put you here.

Now what is the reason for our being? I'm only going to tell you what I think, and if you don't like it, just quietly walk out—don't disturb anyone around you; and if you do like it, just try to think with me about it. Why is Creation? I'm going to tell you what I think: I think it exists for the delight of God. What else can it exist for? Someone will say you are here to get saved. I don't happen to think we are lost, and I know darned well if I *am* lost, there isn't anybody in the world that will know where to look for me. Claptrap, jargon, nonsense, asininity, and confusion—that is all I can think about it right now.

The Universe exists not for us to save our souls—they

are not lost, believe me; nor because the Devil has got us: there isn't any Devil, there isn't any Hell. Somebody said, this morning, "Have you heard from Bill?"* and I said, "Yes." And they said, "Where is he?" and I said, "Just a little south of Hell"—because he is way down there in the tropics. But of course that is just a word picture. There is no Hell, no Devil, no Purgatory; there is no Limbo. This is all nonsense made up by minds who are either vicious or ignorant. But it doesn't add up to anything. It is not sane.

There is a Law of Cause and Effect that beats us up when we beat life up, and will beat the living stuffing out of us until we get tired of it and have had enough and act in accord with the laws of harmony which are fundamental to the nature of God and the Universe in which you and I live. That is why Jesus said, "They that take the sword shall perish with the sword"; "Give, and it shall be given unto you." And Emerson said, "If the red slayer think he slays, / Or if the slain think he is slain, / They know not well the subtle ways / I keep, and pass, and turn again." That is, the Law always moves in a circle.

The Universe must exist for the "glory" of God, in a sense, but really for the Self-expression of God and the delight of God. You and I are born out of It, and we are born out of a divine urge that creates. "The wind bloweth where it listeth, and thou . . . canst not tell whence it cometh, and whither it goeth: so is every one that is born of the Spirit," Jesus said. God is the Spirit; the Spirit seeks; there is a pressure against everything

*William H.D. Hornaday, close associate of Dr. Holmes.

to express life. The dog must bark, the cat must have kittens, the hen must lay eggs, the artist must paint (no matter how terrible it looks), the singer must sing, the dancer must dance: everything must express life. We are born to create, and we can't help it. Why is that? Because God is in us, the great Creator.

Now in psychology they call this the Id and the Libido. It doesn't matter what it is called. *Libido* means an emotional craving back of all things for self-expression, the repression of which leads to psychoneurosis. You may wonder what this has to do with the subject. I am leading up to the subject, and if I don't get to it, it will be too bad. But there is no use choosing a subject unless you can prove there is a principle governing it. My subject is How to Be Happy and Make Others Happy—and, I might add, without wistful wishing or idle dreaming or psychological withdrawing from the realities of life. There is a Law governing these things, and we must understand It, and then we can use It.

We can't help but create. A person who doesn't love something, a person who isn't happy, a person who isn't loved and doesn't make others happy, and others don't make him happy, is unexpressed. Something about him is born and died and going around inside him like a corpse which he is carrying—and we all carry too many of them. There is something unexpressed, and he isn't yet awake and alive and aware of the great realities of life. That is why we miss those whom we love: they open a channel to us. But back of it all, what is happening? God made us out of Himself. Why? There wasn't anything else God *could* make! *God is all there is.* God and nothing,

God plus nothing, leaves nothing but God. "We are born of eternal day / And made in the image of God, / To traverse a heavenly way." We have to love; we have to be loved; we can't be happy without love—we can't be happy without security.

Now there is a pressure against everybody to live, to dance, to sing—and I know, because part of my activity for 45 years is to take people's hair down and see what they look like; I mean their reality: dealing with people where they live. They are all just alike; *we* are all just alike—except each is an individualization, a unique representation. But our emotions, our thoughts, our feelings, our longings, our needs, the needs of the human being: he must love and be loved; he must be happy and make others happy, because he can't be happy unless he does; and back of it all there is the great urge to live.

Now this is back of all modern psychology and psychiatry, and there has been a difference of opinion as to what is the nature of that urge. The original instigators of what is now pretty much modern psychiatry and modern psychology—the three main ones—had three different viewpoints, as you all know. With Freud, it was biological love. With Adler, it was the will to power and personality, and the expression of the Ego. With Jung, it was (and is) that we all represent, dynamically, the history of the whole human race. It is rather a broad-gauged presentation but pretty true coverage. They all have a little different idea, and personally I accept all three.

There is a desire to love and be happy, to give, to receive; back of it all, a necessity to create. Consequently it is known in psychology that the life that does not express the love and joy and receive it buries a lot of its necessary creativity. It can't help it. It is the uncreated life, the uncreative life. We all have more or less of that.

Now it is known definitely that at the back of 85 percent of our physical troubles, *all* of our unhappiness (I think), at least 85 percent of our accidents, and I believe pretty much everything else—I have just told you what has been proven—there is a repression in us: the great creative urge has been sat upon or hasn't found fulfillment, and so it raises all kinds of troubles. It is said that 85 percent of all diseases are because of this—not just by metaphysicians like we are, but by doctors, psychiatrists, psychologists, people who have made a study of it; and there isn't any question but what they are right. Now we *want* to be happy, we are *born* to be happy, we *ought* to be happy, we *should* be happy—but our nature is such that each one of us is an individual creative center in a universal Law of Wholeness and Completion.

There is nothing wrong with God. *We* may be wrong; *we* may suffer (we do); *we* may be impoverished (we are); *we* may be unhappy (we get that way). But we are born to be happy, to be abundantly supplied with every good thing, to have fun in living, to consciously unite with the divine Power that is around us and within us, and to grow and expand forever. "Ever as the spiral grew, / He left the old house for the new"—and we are all Hell-bent for Heaven, whether we believe it or not; and we'll all get there.

Sam Walter Foss* said, "Let the howlers howl / And

*(1858–1911), American editor and humorist.

the growlers growl / And the scowlers scowl, / And let the rough gang go it. / But behind the night / There is plenty of light / And the world is all right, / And I know it." And Jesus said, "Fear not, little flock; it is your Father's good pleasure to give you the kingdom."

Now each one of us is a center in creativity. We want to be happy and we want to make others happy. We don't quite know what is the most important thing. I wish to mention this morning one of the most important things any one of us can learn. (If you don't believe it, please do not reject it, think it over, if it takes you six months.) Would it seem possible to you or to me that the reaction to us of people we meet is unconsciously invited by us, unconsciously drawn to us, by an immutable Law, and held there until we loose it ourselves—? This is the only obsession and the only devils there are. *We* are the obsessing entity, and *we* are the only devil we will ever meet. I don't believe in a Devil, but sometimes I believe in a lot of them. I say I don't believe in any hell we are going to, but I am constrained sometimes to believe in the one we are getting out of. "If I make my bed in hell, behold, thou art there. . . . If I say, Surely the darkness shall cover me, even the night shall be light about me." "Yea, though I walk through the valley of the shadow of death, I will fear no evil, for thou art with me." This we must never forget.

The divine Center, the living Presence, That which you and I did not put there—we didn't have sense enough; we don't quite realize it *is* there. Therefore we live incompletely; but always pressing against the gateway of our consciousness, seeking admission, is That which forevermore sings the song of Its own wholeness, forevermore embraces us. O Love that will not let me go! I believe in It: God is Love.

We are all sensitive. Now the more sensitive you are, the more you pay for it until you are redeemed. Then the better off you are; everything has its price. The more hurt a person gets, the more he can give—the worse he can suffer, and the better off he can be when he learns how to use it. The atomic bomb is very destructive; but that energy "cryptic in Nature, which it has caught like fire from heaven," will some day be the energy that runs all the machinery in the world, shoves every boat across the ocean, every train, every airplane, lifts the water of the sea and distills it as pure as a mountain spring. That is what is going to happen to this cryptic energy, this fire caught from Heaven. But it *could* destroy the world. Let's not be afraid of forces merely because they have been destructively used.

The most destructive force you and I have—and the most constructive—is our own unconscious emotional and thinking and feeling state. Now I am just like you are, and you are just like I am. We are not different —we laugh and cry, we suffer, we get over it, we get tired, we get rested, we fall down and pick ourselves up, we get all messed up and then try to straighten it out. And if it weren't for the goodness of God, we wouldn't last ten minutes, because we haven't that kind of sense. We are all unconsciously trying to commit suicide.

I had a friend once whose husband killed himself; and some person who lacked divine Wisdom, and God knows was without intelligence, said,"He went to a special place reserved for suicides"; and she came in tearing her hair.

She said, "What can I do?" and I said, "Sit down, sister, till I beat some sense into your head. Didn't you know that we *all* commit suicide?" And she said, "How is that?" "Well," I said, "some of us eat too much, some of us drink too much, some smoke too much—and some are just too damned mean to live." Wasn't that terrible? But she is a smart woman, and I beat some plain, common sense into her head, and she went out knowing there was no particular hell with a special rack upon which her beloved husband was roasting. And I said, "We *all* do it sooner or later—because *all* death, so-called, is unnatural. So forget it. Who are we to question the goodness of God, the integrity of the Universe, or the immutable laws of our own being—?"

It is like Walt Whitman, who was kind of lazy like I am—I find lazy people live longer and take it easier; he said, "I loaf and invite my soul." I wonder if you and I do enough loafing. There is a divine Something inside us, of that I am sure. Wouldn't it be terrific—kind of tragic at first, and finally kind of comical, and the most dynamic thing we ever discovered—if we would say, "There is no law but my own soul shall set it under the one great Law of all life." If I am sensitive, if I have lost the object of my love temporarily, yes—I'll cry.* Tears are made to be shed. I'm not afraid of tears, and I think it is a silly person who says he doesn't have to shed them and never feels badly. It isn't true. He is just lying to cover up a great truth, and that will never get him anywhere. This is not daydreaming or escaping from reality.

*This may be an allusion to Dr. Holmes' loss of his wife, Hazel, in May of the preceding year.

We are the most realistic people who ever lived on earth. It is a *transcendental* realism, however. We believe in the transcendence. Now we want love, we want happiness. How, if what I am saying is true—that everything goes out in a circle—if I sit here unhappy, hating everybody, saying the world is against me, which all may be true in appearance—how am I going to draw anything *but* that? I discovered years ago to my own satisfaction that in dream analysis, in psychiatry and psychology—and in a few years it will be proven to be true—the interpretation of dreams is not on a scientific basis at all; because what *is* on a scientific basis—two and two will make four wherever you find them; sugar will be sweet whether it is in a sugar bowl or a dust pan—isn't true of these things, because unconsciously the analyst induces a state, subjectively in his patient, which is like his own conviction so he can interpret his dream. He doesn't know it, but he is planting it there.

The mind unconsciously pictures things and projects them—and says, "Nobody likes me; I am not attractive; nobody loves me; I haven't got what it takes." Now everybody who meets us, meets us psychically—that is, subjectively. He meets us on three levels,* and we can't help it; that is the way we are made. I had a doctor call me up the other day to tell me about a patient, and he said, "Ernest, I know what you believe; but this guy needs certain medical care." And I said, "Wait a minute; I am nobody's fool, and I don't believe I can think a thought that will keep somebody from bleeding if I cut his throat"; and he said, "You're a doll!"—just like that. And I said,

*See below.

"Give me the diagnosis and I'll work *with* you: I *do* believe." And he said, "I do, too." And that is right.

When this thing is put together, it is going to do terrific things. Now whether we know it or not, we live on three planes: man is spirit, soul, and body—or pneuma, psyche, and soma. These are taken from the Greek. *Pneuma* means spirit; *psyche* means mind; and *soma* means body. We meet people on all three planes—spiritual, mental (including psychic), and physical—and we can't help it, because that is the way we are. If there is in us a spiritual transcendence, if there is a universal concept, people will feel it, but they won't know *what* they feel—and that doesn't matter; but they *will* feel it. If there is in us a deep love for everyone—even though, say, it is oversentimental—they will like it. If consciously or unconsciously we are embracing the world, they will know they are included. If we are hurt and sensitive, it will repel people from us.

Now this is why it is. You know and I know in our own experience. We know, by watching others, how terribly sensitive people suffer and seem to repel the very thing they so greatly desire. This is all in accord with the Law. It is the Law that binds the ignorant but frees the wise—like every other law in nature: it binds the ignorant but frees the wise. Moses said that the Law is in your own mouth—a blessing or a curse. The person who is so afraid that people will hurt him and then says all kinds of crazy things, because he is embarrassed, is trying to get somebody to do it. The very effort subjectively flows through the psychic receptivity of the recipient and returns to him with the same unconscious sense of repulsion.

If I am afraid that people won't like me ever, they can't.

171

I have planted in them the dream about me that I am interpreting through them. That is why I spoke about the interpretation of dreams. I know I will be contradicted, but I don't care. I know the time is coming when even in psychiatry and psychology they will say there is only one universal Subjectivity and we use It. There is no such thing as an individual mind at all—there is a *Mind principle*, and we use It. There is a Spirit, and we live by It; and a Law which governs everything, and each one of us has his awareness in It, reacting back to him—because the Universe is one system. This I know.

Now it is mathematically certain to be true: if you are sensitive, if you are hurt, if you are unhappy, you cannot make other people happy, because all that can project from you is sensitiveness, hurt, and unhappiness. It is impossible. Therefore we must rise above it; but we must have a reason for doing so. If I know, and I am 100 percent certain, that every rebuff I get from life is an unconscious reaction of something I have put into my own law, I shall at least for the first time say, "Thank God I now have a key. And no matter how long it takes, I shall arrive!" I know of no other system of thought that teaches it—not in our field or similar fields. Yet Jesus taught it. "Give, and it shall be given unto you." Laugh, and people will laugh with you. Now it is going to be a pretty tough thing. The Truth is not easy always to follow.

I must follow it, though—because I was born as sensitive as anybody ever was—so sensitive that I had a sore throat all the time. I had it swabbed out and out and everything done to it, and it didn't do any good. But after

I got over my sensitiveness, I didn't have it. Sensitiveness is morbid—creates "morbid secretions." I know what it means to be hurt by life; no one knows any better. I have seen the time—and when I was quite young—when I was so hurt I would go to a show because I was alone in a big city, and would have to get up and walk up and down the street to keep from getting so depressed that I thought I would go crazy. Isn't that terrible?

But we are all just alike in these things, and it is nothing to be ashamed of. We don't have to be ashamed if we have a hairlip, you know; we don't have to be ashamed if we have blue eyes. Our psychological confusions are not our fault, they are just things that are happening to us that we must learn about, and they must be corrected —because we *must* be happy; we are *born* to be happy. Now don't worry about making other people happy. If you are happy, you can give what you have got, and if you are not, you can't.

What right do we have to believe that we ought to be happy? We believe in God; we believe in the destiny of the human soul; we believe in the transcendent Presence within us. I caught myself spontaneously saying the other day—I guess it is from the Bible—"I was with You before the world was."* Now I am talking to God without thinking about it, right out loud—in the bathroom—and I said, "I was with You before the world was; I was with *You* before the mountains were made or the sea was formed or the universe was created.† 'The sun across its course

*See John 17:5.
†See Proverbs 8:23–30.

may go, / The ancient river still may flow— / I am and still I am.' I was with You, God, in the beginning—except there wasn't any beginning, just a picture. And what You have made, You know what to do with." I was working on a problem I didn't see the answer to—and I said, "*You* who make all things in me, make *this*; let it be so."

We must start right here: I must be happy. I must find a reason for being happy. I must know that while there appear to be, out there, things that make me unhappy, fortunately I can change them—because finally there shall come to me no kernel of good but the grain I have raised myself, and ground, and baked into the loaf of the bread of Life which I shall eat and share with you. If this were not so, we would be checkerboards, a game of chance, and all life would be a tragedy. And this we cannot attribute to the infinite and ineffable God.

I accept, but it is tough; it is hard. It is realistic. Can a man lift himself by his bootstraps? He can, if he understands what he is doing. Conscious, definite treatment *will* work—coming to see I am one with the Whole Thing; I love everybody; I give to everybody; I am happy; I sing. There is no sadness to the soul. There is something in you and in me that is transcendent of tragedy and sorrow and grief and loss—Power perennially springing from the innermost recesses of that unborn Reality which is evermore being born in us today. This is the glory of our work; this is the power of what we do; this is the Presence of the living Spirit we adore; this is the song we sing. "O living Truth that shall endure / When all that seems shall suffer shock, / Arise on the rock and make me pure."

We have our message to the individual first—to you,

to me: Beloved, you are that Thing which you seek; you are that Thing which you long for. The great and the good and the gracious God exists in you. "Act as though I am" and consciously dissolve those thoughts and feelings and fears; and look out. As Emerson said, "The universe remains to the heart unhurt; the finite alone has wrought and suffered, the Infinite lies stretched in smiling repose." I can say with sincerity, and I believe with certainty, there is an immutable Law of God that can make you happy and make me happy. And because we are happy, people around us will be happy; because we love, they will love us; because we embrace, they will embrace us. To surrender to the dignity of that Law, to the love of that Presence, to the glory and joy of that Being and no longer be afraid of the Universe in which we live . . . "Fear not, little flock, it is your Father's good pleasure to give you the Kingdom."

Let us enter in and possess that Promised Land. Someone might say, "I don't know enough, I am not good enough." I have *told* you enough; and if you are not good enough, neither you nor I can help it. But you *are*! God didn't make a mistake when he made you. You are an exalted being. You are the graciousness of the living God; you are the incarnation and embodiment of the living Spirit; you are the joy of God, you are the delight of God, you are the song of God. But *you* didn't make it, and *you* can't change it. And anyone who will sing a song will hear it come back from a thousand other voices; anyone who will love enough will be loved; anyone who will be happy enough will make happiness, and make others happy. He can't help it.

If It were out *there*; if I had to wait for the vicissitudes of fortune, good or ill; then It would be a reed shaken by the wind. But if there is an integrity within me, shall I not have the patience and courage and fortitude at long last to look up into the face of the eternal Life in which I live, and say, "God, I thank you, that *I* gave birth to every trouble I ever had and every sadness and every fear"—? I know what tears are as well as you—because if I didn't, I should be in the clutch of extraneous forces from which there would be no escape. But the soul is free and the Spirit is boundless. "Thou hast made us—Thine we are." I was with Thee before ever the world was born, or the mountains or the sea or the sky, and I will be with Thee when the belief in a material universe shall be rolled up like a scroll and laid away in the archives of men's memory.

I am that which Thou art, O living Truth. I am that which Thou art. So the key is here. Should we not be enthusiastic? Should we not be joyful, even though we are stilll burdened with our previous mistakes? And at long last—too long!—I have counted my seven times over and over; but seven times one are seven. The dreary monotony, the hopeless anguish, the sleepless nights, the tears that were shed and unshed, the cry of the heart—why? How long, O God? And then the answer, as a sun rises across a new horizon, as the birds sing, as the laughter of children comes to the years and the hope and the heart: "I was with thee before the world was—in love, in joy; and My world shall be joy and love." Lord God of Heaven and Earth, my God forevermore. Amen.

AFFIRMATIVE-PRAYER MEDITATION

(Now we have a lot of names in here; different people want different things to happen in their experience. Each person who has put his name in here knows what he wants to happen. He will specialize what we are believing; that is, he will identify himself with the result of his desire, as though it were already accomplished. Now this is following the pattern of Jesus, who said, "When you pray, believe you have it." The experiments they made at Redlands, and all metaphysical work which is an affirmation made in the present: it now is this way; it has been proven and demonstrated this is the way to do it: "When ye pray, believe you have it, and you shall receive."

(So the persons will believe; and you and I, working with them and for them in our own consciousness, will know that each and every name that appears here represents the living Presence of the eternal God, the embodiment of the living Spirit, the perfect Life.)

There is one Life, It is God, It is this person's life now, whoever it may be. He is under the government of That; he is directed, guided. Everything this man does shall prosper. He knows what to do and how to do it and receives the impulsion to do whatever he ought to. There isn't a thing about his activity that he doesn't know. Any person he ought to meet, he will; any information he ought to receive, he will receive. New ideas, new thoughts, new things, new friendships, new situations, new conditions are coming to him, flowing joyously. His mind receives them; he is glad.

There is no past, no sin, no condemnation; there is no judgment: we are wiping that out. God has not made any mistakes in him—he is all right, and he knows it. "In joy shall he drink from the well of salvation." Joy and love and friendship shall accompany him—that is all that goes out, that is all that comes back. He is guided; he is prospered: everything he does shall prosper. It is prospering now, multiplying. He gives and he receives and he is blessed.

And for every person who has asked for a physical healing, let us know his body is a divine Pattern: God has made it. "Thou hast made us; Thine we are." And in this moment our recognition of the Presence of the living Spirit makes whole and new every organ, every action, and every function of his body, circulation, assimilation, elimination—it is a body of divine ideals and ideas and truths and realities. It is in harmony with the infinite Pattern which has created and sustains it. This word is the law of elimination to everything that contradicts that.

And now shall love and joy and gladness and the longing of the heart and companionship of life fulfill the aspiration and feeling, and meet the needs of the daily life. There is nothing wrong with us; we were born to be whole and happy. And now as we silently bless this person, he is indeed blessed;

and as we turn to the great heart of Love in and around us and recognize the divine nature of our own being and consciously unify ourselves with the living Spirit, we thank God. And as we look at each other, we behold there the living Presence, love and friendship, and joy forever and forevermore.

CHAPTER 11

You Are a Spiritual Broadcasting Station

O UR SUBJECT THIS morning is "You Are, or Might
Become, a Spiritual Broadcasting Station."* Now
this is either true or it isn't true; and if it is true, it is one
of the most startling facts the human mind can conceive
relative to human relations, whether we know it or not
or believe it or not: that we are automatically broadcasting, sending out influence, thought, feeling—something
that on its plane is tangible. Then this is one of the most
remarkable things we could consider; because somewhere
in the aura—that is, in the extent of this atmosphere
which surrounds us and is created by us without our
knowing it—exists sickness and health (most of it), poverty and wealth, love and friendship. And because I am
long-winded, the second half of this talk will be given
next Sunday morning.

You just can't give this sort of thing in 30 minutes—
because we *teach* something. We don't preach; we *teach*.
We have no "healers" in our movement and no prophets.

*See "You Are a Spiritual Broadcasting Station," pp. 270–275 of Dr.
Holmes' book *Living the Science of Mind,* for a different treatment
of this subject.

"There are no prophets other than the wise." No one has a healing power, any more than someone has electricity. He can have an upset liver, but he cannot *have* a healing power: he *uses* one. Who has gravitational force? He has a freedom in a field of gravitational force.

Now if you and I are spiritual broadcasting stations, then this broadcast is automatic and unconscious most of the time: we don't even know it is there, but it is working. "And seeing the multitudes, he went up into a mountain; and when he was set, his disciples came unto him; and he opened his mouth, and taught them, saying, . . . Blessed are the pure in heart: for they shall see God." This is the beginning of the Sermon on the Mount and the Beatitudes—the greatest spiritual discourse, probably, the world has ever received.

A *mount* stands for a consciousness of transfiguration—a high estate of consciousness. I take it that "Blessed are the pure in heart: for they shall see God" must mean that there is a certain attitude of thought, of mind in consciousness where the divine Presence is revealed to us in the things we look at and in the people we contact. Jesus must have meant this. He didn't mean we would see what the artists have depicted as an old man with long whiskers, sending thunderbolts to the Methodists and sugar candies to the Baptists, etc. There is no God, fortunately, who knows anything about our little idiosyncrasies and our puny efforts toward salvation. Someone said they were sorry they brought someone to hear me the other Sunday because his friends were Baptists. Now I used to be a Baptist, and they are nice people; and no one need be ashamed that he is a Baptist. And if he has been baptised, he needn't be ashamed of the rite—it is beautiful and very sweet. But if he thinks there is any salvation in being ducked, he is screwy.

I always say, "I thank the God that *is*, that the God that is believed in, *isn't*." "Blessed are the pure in heart: for they shall see God." Where will they see God? In each other; everywhere: in the tree, in the burning bush. They shall hear Him in the song of the birds, in children at play. They shall really see God wherever they look, wherever their vision is set. "As thou seest, / That thou be'st; / As thou beholdest, man, / That too become thou must: / God if thou seest God, / Dust, if thou seest dust."

Who has had vision enough to look for God, try to see God everywhere, stayed with it long enough? Only the man who has done that could deny what Jesus affirmed; and the man who *has* done it, *won't* deny it. And the people who haven't done it, don't know anything about it; and we shouldn't be worried if they think we are kind of screwy. So what! Who should worry what anyone thinks, if we have demonstrated to ourselves something that makes life more complete—?

Now we are broadcasting stations. Do you remember a woman came up back of Jesus and touched the hem of his garment and was immediately made whole; and he turned around and said, "I perceive that power has gone out of me . . . your faith has made you whole."

Vincent Sheean in a book called *Lead Kindly Light*—which is a story of the life of Gandhi, whom he knew—says that when Gandhi sat with even 2 or 3 million people, farther out than you could see—a sea of faces, an ocean of people—there was established between him and these people what they called *Darshan*. It is something that communicates itself between the audience and the speaker, and the speaker and the audience. I have always felt it; I can tell when it begins to happen with an audience. I have always thought of it as a kind of triangle—I don't know why; but *here* the speaker is, *there* the audience is, and something else is formed *up here* which flows back to each one, accentuated and multiplied. I am sure every speaker feels it and every audience does: a communication is established.

Now down here at the university where Dr. Parker* teaches in the Department of Psychology and Philosophy, they established that you can bless plants, as you know, or curse them or tell them they are good or no good; and they will respond—and at a distance. This is not something that happened in the corner of the earth that couldn't be demonstrated. It is so! It has been known for a long time that there are people who could take this watch, and could see George† in the watch crystal—and they had never seen him before. Now he wouldn't really be in there; it is like people looking into a crystal ball: there isn't anything in the crystal ball, you know; but they use it as an instrumentality. *They would see him.*

It is called *psychometry*. It is in the realm of the psychic sciences. A brick that was in the house of Julius Caesar—they would describe the house; and if they are clairvoyant, they might see people going back and forth; and if they are clairaudient, they might hear their voices of 2000 years ago. It is possible for anyone under a certain psychic condition to "remember" anything that ever

*William Parker, co-author of *Prayer Can Change Your Life.*
†George Bendall, close associate of Dr. Holmes.

happened to anyone who ever lived, if they tune into the vibration of that person's consciousness as it then was, because nothing has happened to it as it now is; because time has no existence in this medium.

All these things are true, because they have been demonstrated and demonstrated over and over again. We are all emitting some kind of an atmosphere. You have often gone into a home and sat down and wished you weren't there—you feel irritated and fidgity and want to scream. *I* have, and I don't scream very much—and then other places you say, "I would like to sit down here!" I met a woman the other day who is about six feet tall, and someone asked how I liked her, and I said, "She is the kind of person I feel I could sit in her lap and be rocked to sleep." She is that motherly type. Someone else ruffles us and we think, How did *you* get in here?!

This is the real thing. The aura is the mental atmosphere around us. You can even see it: sometimes it is light and sometimes it is dark. It varies. When a person is angry, it is like flashes of lightning. It can be heavy or light. Now we are all familiar with these things; but everyone didn't know it is possible to see these things and hear them; but it is. So we are all broadcasting something. I read not too long ago in *Pageant Magazine* or some popular one about a man who gets up feeling very happy and jolly, gets in a streetcar to go somewhere, sits down beside somebody, and begins to feel morose and unhappy and sad and wishes he were dead—and he discovers this other man is in a very depressed state. He sits in the atmosphere of depression. That is a broadcast.

These things are not imaginary. But you know, they

are so startling, so dramatic, so fraught with intense meaning that if we really quite understood what it would be like, we should naturally want to broadcast that which is good and true and beautiful. You know, if everybody gets to believe in a new-fangled kind of disease, most everybody gets it. Doctors know this. This is no criticism of doctors: they know it better than you and I. We cooperate with physicians. I often ask a doctor, if I am treating anyone, to give me a diagnosis and tell me what ought to happen for the patient to be better so I can treat that it *will* happen. I have no superstitions; I don't believe in any devil or hell, etc., or future punishment. There is no God who is going to add insult to injury. I just kind of believe in God and nothing else.

I think we are living in a Spiritual Universe governed by mental laws, or Intelligence acting as Law; and I think each one of us is surrounded by the atmosphere or aura of his own thinking and his own background. Way back in there, as Carl Jung says, is the whole world. That is the mortal mind or carnal mind or collective mind—doesn't matter what you call it; and we are all attracting or repelling, according to the atmosphere; and we are all broadcasting this atmosphere.

There are people who are so self-conscious, so self-critical, so effacing of themselves that even in company you can feel a sense of rejection around them. You know these things as well as I do. It isn't conscious: they didn't plan it that way; God knows they didn't want it that way. There are people who are so lonely you can feel their loneliness. There are people so impoverished you can almost smell the odor of poverty. Please don't think I am screwy. These things are true. They are amazing. But it would *have* to be that way, because the Universe in which we live is that way. God is an infinite Mind.

I think we all live in an infinite Mind, and our thoughts go into It and surround us, and then they attract or repel; but they are always influencing everything they touch. Now we know that everything has an atmosphere. It isn't going to be very long before they can take a splinter out of this podium (whatever they call it) and send it to London and they will take a picture of this podium. They will tune the camera into the vibration that is going around the world from everything and returning—because all energy returns to its source with the speed of light; and that would be 7½ times in a second. The camera would tune into this particular object because the splinter from this object would tune it into *it*. Then all they would have to do is take a picture in that vibration and they would have this podium.

Don't think this is funny. They are almost doing it now —and doing things that are proving this principle: just with a drop of your blood, taking a picture of the internal organs and the soft tissue. I have seen it done. And sometimes when I mention this, people say, "Don't say such things, Ernest; people will think you are crazy"; and I say, "Isn't that grand! What difference does that make? *I have seen it done!*"

The Universe is a little different than we think it is; but the practical result of this thing is terrific. It means that whether you and I know it or not, whenever anyone thinks about us, they are not exactly tuned into our innermost life, but they *are* tuned into the periphery of that which extends itself, no matter where they are on earth;

and this explains most clairvoyance. I am not denying clairvoyance—because it is true. Now don't laugh; this is true, and I have seen it—and I don't drink very much! (But if I did, it would not be anybody's business.)

You see, we are not reformers; and do you know *why* we are not reformers? Because we never got *ourselves* reformed. And anybody who *gets* himself reformed won't try to reform anybody else—because he will be free. Someone has said, "Life is a comedy to him who thinks, a tragedy to him who feels." I am not a reformer; so I don't even know how to tell you how to pray. Emerson said, "When that divine moment comes, leave all of your theories as Joseph left his coat in the hands of the harlot, and flee." No one can tell me what is right for *me*. I know. And even if what I "know" as right is *wrong*: it is "right" for me when I *think* it is right; and I will have to suffer by it until I *get* it right; else I would be an automaton.

At any rate, whether we believe it or not, every time anyone thinks of us, he tunes in to some part of us, he tunes into what we are broadcasting. He can't help it. Now this is true from the farthermost ends of the earth —because of this subtle emanation, whatever it may be; *I* don't know. I read not too long ago some very eminent scientist said a brick is different than we thought it was. He said there is a flow through this brick and an emanation from it around the world like the speed of light, and back to it. It is more than a *solid fact*: it is a *fluidic emanation*. How much more so this is in the realm of Mind!

Now we would like to feel—*I* would—that everyone we touch is made happy and whole. I tried a very interesting experiment last February when I went back to

Florida. I had spoken a couple of times in Miami, but I spoke in four cities this time. I had never been in them and didn't know the people. The only thing I treated for all day on the way there was that I loved these people. I don't *know* them, but I *love* them—because I think love is the only security there is in the Universe. There is nothing worthwhile without it; and with it, a person can live —even if he has nothing else. We *must* have love, and for *everybody*. I'll bet I had a hundred people say to me, "It must be wonderful to be loved the way you are!" I never treated anybody would love me. I treated *I* would love *them*. But you see, the thing goes out on a circuit and it comes back on a circuit. "Give, and unto you it shall be given; good measure, pressed down, and shaken together, and running over, shall men press it into your hands."

Now antagonism is broadcast; overcritical attitudes are broadcast; coldness, disdain are broadcast. We feel these people, shake hands with people only to embrace them in our thought or push them away from us mentally. You do it and I do it and everyone does it. We can't help it. I know we would all like to be a blessing to everything we touch; we should like to bring peace and joy to every situation; we should like to bring encouragement and love and confidence and security and sympathy and compassion. We should like to broadcast it—so that everyone who thinks of me will think, He is a wonderful guy. What is wrong with that? I'd rather have someone think I am a wonderful guy than that I am what some people get called who are not wonderful guys.

What is wrong in wanting people to like you? I don't see anything wrong; I don't think it is a bloated ego.

What are we here for? There is nothing wrong with the ego; it is what we have done *to* it and *with* it. It is a very valuable thing, and if we didn't have it, we wouldn't be here; there wouldn't be "anybody at home."

There is no God who is trying to curse us. We don't think half well enough of ourselves. You are the most wonderful thing you will ever meet, and I am the most wonderful thing I'll ever meet—but I do amuse myself; and I like that, too—and we are the only person we are ever going to have to live with throughout eternity; and we are going to attract or repel according to what we are. Of course, we ought to find out how to broadcast that which is worthwhile.

Now it is very simple. We have to love, if we are going to broadcast love. We can't hate and broadcast love any more than this harp will broadcast the piano. Kind after kind—everything reproduces its own kind always. That is the way Nature is. Now when the woman came up and touched Jesus and was healed, it was because there was such a consciousness of wholeness within him, and of givingness and of love, that the moment she entered it she felt it. It operated through her and healed her.

No one knows yet what would happen right in an audience like this if enough people knew it was going to happen. It would break down all resistance, dissolve all apparent solidness, and heal, I believe, everyone—and beyond that bring joy and comfort and assurance and love to the saddened heart. That is what we all need. It is nice to have money when you need it, nice to be free from pain; but it is more wonderful to have no fear and no uncertainty and have confidence in the Universe and love for each other and a depth of feeling that will not be disturbed. Tennyson said of the Lady of the Lake, symbolizing a state of consciousness, "She is calm, whatsoever storms assail the sea, and when the tempest rolls, has power to walk the waters like our Lord." "And Jesus stilled the waves."

Now we want to broadcast this. *I* do. I'd like to know that if I pass through a situation, it is healed; if I am in a group of people, I love them and they love me and we embrace each other. I'd like to know that everybody who thinks of me feels a newness of life. That isn't ego. We are all inlets to God, Emerson said, and may become outlets. God made us inlets; we will have to make ourselves outlets.

How wonderful it would be to feel we silently bless everyone we touch and everyone who thinks of us! There is so much in what you and I believe and understand that I have said to George several times and others around me: we are playing around on the fringe of the great miracle of Life. We are on the shores of an infinite Ocean. Sometimes we feel the spray in our face, the waves lapping our feet; but how seldom do we plunge beneath Its depth!

We ought to broadcast beauty. I am a great lover and almost worshipful adorer of beauty—the harmony, the symmetry. I love to see people who do the best they can with whatever it is they have. I don't think a woman is conceited because she gets her face lifted and dresses the best she can; I think she is silly if she *doesn't* look the best she can—or a man too. Why do we want to pull a long face, as though we said to the world, "Look at me and drop dead." This terrific morbidity, this awful condemnation, is a load that must be lifted; it is a weight on the brow of progress; it saddens the heart. And whoever is so stupid as to believe it is imposed upon us—all we have to do is say, "Screwy! Forget it!"—he has a God I don't believe in.

But God comes in the still small voice, in the silent sanctuary of the heart, in the love we bear to each other —"love so infinite, deep, and broad / That men have renamed it and called it God." And I'd rather sit beside a person who loves than sit in the companionship of kings. As Emerson said, if we haven't it, "something writes 'Thou Fool' across the forehead of the king." And the simplest may have it. Almost all children have it. Practically all animals have it—and they smell the scent of fear and attack, because we are afraid of them; they smell fear and attack us in self-protection. That is how it was the lions did not harm Daniel.

Love is a coverage, joy is a grace, peace is a depth of the soul; and there is a song in the heart, even if you haven't any voice to sing it. A mute could sing it. There is an interior awareness which comprehends and embraces all things. We don't have to wonder whether the thing shall come back to us on "the eternal circuits of God." It *will*. We do not have to wonder whether it shall go out. It *must*. We don't have to wonder whether other people sense it. They cannot help it; they *do*; and they react to it. And we are the broadcasting station.

I have broadcast so much in my life; and I know I do some little thing here to myself, somebody hears it, and out there they get what is "in here." It is so with life. Wherever we go, we are met by the return circuit of our own broadcast. Wherever we are, we must drink of the cup we have handed to our fellow men. Whatever we have loved shall love us, whatever we have cursed shall curse us—because the Universe is just, without judgment, without malice. How wonderful to think you and I— unknown to the world (that doesn't matter); uncrowned, unhonored, and unsung (that does not matter)—have within us the possibility of the limitless reaches of Reality! Just a different kind of a broadcasting station: singing day and night, it never stops; dancing night and day, it never stops; loving, living, giving, receiving, light-bearing—for there is a Light that lighteth every man's path, and you are that Light, and I am that Light; and in that Light there is no darkness. Wonderful! We are the broadcasting station and we are the announcer, and the world is the receiver: some kind of an infinite wave more subtle than the waves of the ether that transmit the messages of TV and radio broadcasting. Instant and subtle, automatically success or failure, love or hate, joy or grief, Heaven or Hell—whatever it is that we would be.

I know you would rather bless everything you touch. "Bless the Lord, O my soul, and all that is within me, bless His holy name." How simple! Joy: there is a joy which each of us may have. Peace: "Peace I leave with you, my peace I give unto you; not as the world giveth, give I unto you. Let not your heart be troubled, neither let it be afraid." "Ye believe in God, believe also in me. In my Father's house are many mansions; if it were not so, I would have told you." That simple trust, that child-like faith, that everlasting peace—something deep welling up within our nature forevermore proclaiming the celestial day and time of eternal dawn. Love, and the world will love you; they will make an exception to you. Howsoever foolish, they will feel it. They know. Bring gladness from the heart, and the world will seek you out. But weep, and you weep alone.

This lesson everyone must learn. Within *me*: the adequate Cause, the eternal Presence, the everlasting day— little me, humble me, unpretentious me. O Lord God of Heaven and earth, we are grateful that that which was brought at earliest dawn shall re-sing itself in our heart, and in joy go forth to bless the world.

AFFIRMATIVE-PRAYER MEDITATION

(Now we have a very sweet duty to perform, and that is to use our consciousness on behalf of whoever has put his or her name, for whatever need they may have, in this box in faith and in confidence—with a little longing, perhaps, and a little apprehension and fear, perhaps; I don't know; but as we return to the God within us, we are broadcasting to the God within everyone whose name is here.)

"Listen, God!" (God is speaking to God, and God is answering to God—in this celestial conversation and communion—that every person whose name is here shall be blessed and *is* blessed, beloved of His Spirit.) "We are recognizing Your presence in him, in every organ and action and function of his body, that it shall be whole. It *is* whole." (We are talking to God, the God of wholeness—never had anything wrong with Him and never will; the God who never made a mistake, cannot, and will not; living Truth.)

We are blessing every person here in health and in

joy; let him know the Spirit within him performs the miracle of life. And here upon the altar of our conviction we lay down every doubt and uncertainty and behold His face only, shining as an eternal light. Blessed are the pure in heart, for they *do* see God: we see Him in each one here. Divine guidance is telling everyone here what to do; and if he has a problem, let it be solved. Divine Intelligence knows all things and does all things. Let joy come to him, and Love and Truth and Beauty, and the Light of Heaven light his pathway—as It shall.

Now let each think deep within himself, say to the eternal Presence, "I am that which Thou art, Thou art that which I am, eternal God. All the joy and all the peace there is, and all the energy and action and enthusiasm and creativity there is, is in me—because God is here." Each is saying to himself, "I am one with infinite calm; I am one with all the Power and Joy of the Universe; I am one with the wind and wave and mountain and the desert and my neighbor, children at play, and birds aloft winging their way across the blue of the sky, the sunset and the sunrise, and all things. 'I am that which Thou art, Thou art that which I am' forever and forevermore. Amen."

And now eternal God, everlasting Father, giver and keeper of life, to whom is glory and power and dominion both now and forevermore: we rest in Thee. Amen.

CHAPTER 12

Love: the Law That Attracts Friends

NEXT SUNDAY we start a series on How to Use the Power Greater than We Are. There *is* a Power greater than we are, and we can use It. We know It is there and know how to use It. Anyone in our day and age who is not availing himself of the opportunity of using It is missing something. There is a spiritual Presence we may enjoy, and a Law of Mind in action we may use that is actual and real and works.

We base all of our authority not on anything *I said*, but on what *you do*. I don't care what *I* said, because— much of it I would like to forget. I base any authority of what I said on what you right here *do* with what I said. We have no other authority, ask for none other, need none other, and want no other. They asked Jesus one time: "By what authority do you do it?" And he said, "How do *you* do it? But I'll show you. I'll tell this man to arise, take up his bed, and walk." Now unless there are signs following our conviction, we have no authority. We are just mumbling empty words to ourselves; might be wistful wishing, idle daydreaming, or a monotonous repetition of unmeaningful prayers. *Jesus was very explicit.*

There are two outstanding things about the life of Jesus. First of all, he forgave people their sins and said there is nothing in the Universe that holds anything against you. I have a bad sense of humor sometimes. I wonder what would happen if Jesus were here and listened to the anathemas that are directed to people in his name. It would be very interesting and makes me think of a story that was written by one of our great writers. A carload of people were suddenly shuffled out of this sphere into another one. It was another type of civilization, didn't belong to this world. One of these people was a reformer, and he found that everybody in this other world was naked; so he immediately started a reform. Now these people were very far advanced in civilization, and they didn't beat his brains out. The quietly took him to their psychiatric ward to see why he had such a dirty mind. *They* didn't! That will apply in this world too. (Guess I better begin to pray.)

Let's think of it: what accusations we project at others in criticism are merely unredeemed territories of our own inward morbidities. Today we are going to talk on love and friendship. The Bible says, "Who knows not love knows not God; for God is love." It says, "Though I speak with the tongues of men and of angels, and have not love, I am as sounding brass, or a tinkling cymbal." Browning said, "O heart, O blood that freezes, blood that burns—earth's returns for whole centuries of folly, noise, and sin: shut them in with their triumphs and their glories and the rest. Love is best."

Two of our modern psychiatrists, one of them associated with Dr. Peale,* have written books—one called *Love against Hate*, in which he proves that love is a principle in the Universe, the other called *Love or Perish*. Now this leads us to suppose that God is Love: whatever the impulsion of the Universe is, it is love, beneficence; it is kindness, it is compassion; it is sweetness, truth, beauty—friendly toward us. Now we know, psychologically, that the very first need of man is to love and be loved. We know this; there is no guesswork about it. *They* say it a different way: they say the first law of the libido is it must have an object, and the second law is the ego must not be rejected. That is psychology and psychological terminology. All it means is that everybody has to love, and the love has to be returned or we are not happy.

It is a simple proposition: everyone must love and be loved or he won't be fulfilled or happy. Therefore it is believed that love looses the greatest energy in the Universe—the greatest spiritual energy—and without love there is a certain part of life that does not come to fulfillment. This is real; it is dynamic; it isn't just a sweet sentimentality. If I wish to bring the world to the brink of a place where it is entirely possible for it to annihilate itself: wouldn't that be a travesty, irony of fate? I don't think it is going to; and if it does, it will be all right with me, because we are all going to shuck off this mortal coil some time, and I don't see that it makes any great difference when.

Love didn't do that. Who do we remember in history?

---

*Norman Vincent Peale, clergyman and author of *The Power of Positive Thinking*.

197

Alexander the Great, who at the age of around 30 was so dissatisfied that there were no new things to conquer—? Do you remember Caesar, Hannibal, Napoleon—except that they are dark spots on the pages of history?

No. We remember Jesus and Buddha and Socrates. We remember the great lovers of the human race. Isn't that interesting! Instinctively, then, love seeks its own, and there is no fulfillment without it. Consequently, emotionally, psychologically—and actually in reality—love is the only final security on earth. Now I am not saying this as just a sweet little guy who says, "Look at me and die." I am not doing that. This is *true*. I must accept it because it is a scientific fact. But we knew it before science proved it. Love is the only final security in the Universe; love is the greatest healing power in the Universe, and the only thing that binds people together in a community of Spirit. Therefore love is pretty important in our lives. We cannot pass it off with an idle gesture and say, "The sentimental fool!"

Love is the only security. It is the healing Power, it is the great Reality—"a love so infinite, deep, and broad / That men have renamed it and called it God." Now psychiatry, science, medicine, experience, the intuition of the poet, and the application of our Principle tell us this. Let's accept it and see what we can do about it.

Love—just plain love; liking everybody. We are so constituted that real love is real only in such degree as it is universal. I am not talking just about a love that says, "God bless me and my wife, my son John and his wife, we four and no more." That isn't love—it is selfishness; establish the fact philosophically and scientifically, because then it will be a spiritual fact. In other words, we want to know *what is so*. Now we do know: we have to love, and we have to be loved. We must feel wanted, needed, and loved. We must have friendship. We must have our arms around each other.

Some people will say this is silly, this is sentimental. That's all right. I have watched the world twirl around quite a while, and I have observed it pretty carefully, and in nearly half a century I have counseled with so many thousands; and I'll say this: I have never yet seen a person who is unsentimental, who hasn't that compassion and that kind of fulfillment—I don't care how smart he is; he might be very intellectual in his attainment.

I have never seen one single one of them that seemed very far removed from a stone image. I could hug any person here and love it, but I could not embrace a stone image—it is too unrelenting and doesn't respond. There is something in animals that knows whether you like them or not. I have never had a dog even snap or growl at me, because I love them. I never have had trouble getting along with children. Someone said yesterday that where they were going to rent a place they were asked if there were children. I said, "If it were me, I would love it if there were a dozen kids on each side of the apartment; I would love to hear them yell. There is something about it that makes me feel good inside."

Psychologically, that means this is regression and I am returning to the days of my youth. That is going to be good. You know, the Bible says if one man in a thousand shall go forth and teach man his uprightness, he shall return unto the days of his youth and his flesh shall become as a little child.* I have never seen anybody terrifically happy who is too prosaic—and remember this: as

*Job 33:23–25.

much as we admire and believe in modern science, which has given us all the comforts of life (and clothes for men that are so uncomfortable for this time of year it ought to be against the law to wear them), one of the things modern science has done is *exclusion*; and all exclusiveness shuts out more than it shuts in. A child knows whether you love him; he feels the confidence of love. I had a child brought to me a couple of weeks ago, about 7 years old. There was a pretty tough situation in the home, and they said, "Shall we bring the child?" and I said, "All right"; and after a few moments I said, "Let the child go out." After I had talked to the adults, finally I said, "You get out and let me talk to the child." He comes over and climbs up in my lap and begins to pat me. He doesn't do that to them: he is afraid of them.

I read where a Sunday School teacher said to a class, "Why did not the lions destroy Daniel?" and they all had an answer; but one little boy said, "I know! They were not afraid of Daniel!" Isn't that putting it in reverse? Everyone else would have said *Daniel* was not afraid of *them*, which is also true. Somebody has written a little book called *The Scent of Fear*, in which it says that the animal attacks us because it smells the odor of fear emanating from our physical being but originating in our emotional reaction. It is a thing of thought, as everything else is.

Love is the lodestone of life. We want friends: I am not trying to tell you how to influence people; that is not the way it is done. *You just don't antagonize people;* that is the way it is done; and they like you. We don't say, "I want this person to be my friend." Now there are certain handicaps (we are "fearfully and wonderfully made").

One of our troubles is we sometimes get to like people so well, and get so afraid that the affection may not be returned, that we become so self-conscious that we are not even normal with them and everything hurts our feelings. We magnify everything and call *criticism* something that is just a *comment*. Therefore to truly love and be loved, we must heal ourselves of fear, of sensitivity—because I happen to believe that most of that sensitive reaction from others we are unconsciously planting there. We have to become whole ourselves. We have to dwell on the thought of love and friendship.

I think in the background of our thoughts should always be "I love you. I love you." One of my closest friends happens to be a professional person, and every time she calls up, when she gets through she says, "I love you." And I say, "I love you too."' That is the way it ought to be. Why are we so afraid of a little sentimentality? Who cares what "they" think?! You know, I have met so many people, from presidents down to paupers and from intellectual geniuses to morons, and I have never met "them" or seen one of "them" who are referred to as in "What will 'they' think?" or "What will 'people' say?" I have never met one of these persons in my life. It is a fictitious assumption.

I was talking to some people at a little party, and one of the men said, "I don't like to drink"; and I said, "Why *do* you?" And he said, "What do you think—when you go to a party and *everyone* drinks!" And I said, "No one will condemn you if you refuse it; you are only condemning yourself. Don't feel self-conscious about *anything* you do. Don't be afraid of life; don't be afraid of people, or of anything. 'Perfect love casteth out fear': it is the only security there is." And I said, "If you think rightly, every-one you know will make an exception to you. They do to me. You are the only great person you are ever going to meet; so start in with not having self-love but self-appreciation. I believe your real ego is the only medi-ary between you and the Absolute that you will ever dis-cover and that it is your spiritual guide and double and the most terrific and wonderful thing anyone ever thought of. Socrates called it his *daemon*.*

I know it is there in everyone. We have to stop being afraid of life and of people; we have to have a decent respect for ourselves. There is a spiritual self: it dominates everything when we let it. There is apparently a pressure against everything—to sing, to dance, to love, and to appreciate, and to join with people; and people are sore and hungry for love—and we all are—so that I think we ought to embrace the whole world in our thought and feeling. I do it definitely and consciously every day—try to stretch my imagination. I thought, if I was too busy for everything else, still I would want to take a few minutes to do this every day before I go to bed at night or, some-times, when I wake up in the morning; it doesn't matter when.

I call it stretching the mind, stretching the intellect, and I just let go and think of a few people I think a great deal of, and I embrace them in my own consciousness; and then I go out, and out, and finally in my imagination I try to get my arms around the world and kind of squeeze it, kind of press it to me. Somebody may say, "You senti-mental fool!"; but I would just as soon be a sentimental

*From the Greek, *daimon*: a power or spirit; genius.

fool. I have met so many fools who are unsentimental and didn't even get any kick out of it. So if we are all going to be fools, let's have sense enough to be *happy* fools.

I am not afraid of the greatest sentiment, the eternal God and the everlasting Spirit instilled as the high motivating Power of man—and without it, the blind shall be leading the blind; and without love, the world can destroy itself. It is the only wholeness that there is.

Now I am not thinking of love as sacrifice and duty. Those who do things out of duty had just as well not do them—they are bloodless wretches. We don't do anything for duty. Supply the word *duty* with *privilege* and *spontaneity*. You don't love your children and your friends because it is a *duty*—you love them because you are not whole until you do. It seems to me it starts with the self: not selfish love but self-realization, self-appreciation. You are the most wonderful thing you will ever meet.

Someone might say this is terrible—*God* is the most wonderful. But Jesus had the courage to say, "Who hath seen me hath seen the Father. . . . Believe that I am in the Father, and the Father in me; or else believe me for the very works' sake." "Whatsoever things the Son seeth the Father do, that doeth the Son also." . . . "that the Father may be glorified in the Son." "The Father hath delivered all things unto the Son." Dont be afraid to *claim*. This is what I call the great claim that your soul makes on God. It is the greatest claim you and I can ever make—that at long last we shall say, "Thank God that I now realize that God is what I am!"

Now this is not selfishness, because very soon we discover we have to include more territory. If I am one with God, so are you; therefore in that Unity which we have and are and enjoy, we have to embrace each other or we are not fulfilling our own nature. If I am one with God and you are one with God, we are each one with God in one field; and until we are one with each other, there isn't the complete delivery of God. This is why Emerson said, "Nature forevermore screens herself from the profane."

Isn't it terrible if a person feels lonely and alone, and lacking in friendship and love, which every person should have! I am a great believer that people who are at *any* age should seek companionship. It isn't silly if a man and woman 80 or 90 get married: it is *sensible*. It just shows that what I am saying is true: love is the lodestone of life—companionship, a feeling of belonging, wanting and needing each other. There is nothing wrong with it; we are wrong if we *don't* seek it. But we discover that we have to take in more territory.

And isn't it wonderful if you can say to somebody who is alone:

Just you begin to think of yourself, first of all, as one in God. Make it simple. *God is all there is.* God is an infinite Presence, a divine Person, a universal Responsiveness: you can talk to God; Something will answer. We don't call God an abstraction or mathematical principle: God is a *Presence*, full of warmth and color and light and awareness—and alive. And awake. There *is* Something in the Universe. And then say, "I am one with This; It is one with me; It is what I am. I am one with all people: every person is my friend. I enjoy the love and friendship; I give the love and friendship and feel one"—just this simple way. Don't try to make it hard; don't say the 23rd Psalm!

All the disciples were great men; but we never met them, and we *have* met *each other*. We will get more out of each other than we will out of Moses. He did well for his day, but behold: we—just little funny you and myself—can look at each other and laugh at each other and embrace each other and love each other; and unless we do, that which is the essence of love will not be delivered.

Every place that we withhold it, we shut out the essence. And where we turn to; where we think we want it from a dearly beloved; we are always unsatisfied. It is back of every jealousy, every domestic problem. You can counsel with them and pray *with* them and *for* them—I believe in all of it, particularly praying *on* them—*but* when all is said and done, the proposition is personal, the problem is personal, and it is so very simple that only childlike words will explain it.

"And he took a little child and said, 'God is like this.'" And they said the children were disturbing him, and he said, "No, suffer the little children to come unto me and forbid them not, for of such is the Kingdom of God." And the wisest man who ever lived—the greatest revelator of spiritual Truth who ever lived*—said, "Don't be afraid to be a child."

As I have said to you before, the poet said: "Turn backward, turn backward, O Time in thy flight / And make me a child again, just for tonight." "Heart weary of building and spoiling, / And spoiling and building again. / And I long for the dear old river, / Where I idled my youth away; / For a dreamer lives forever, / And a toiler dies in a day."

Keep it simple. It is not psychological regression. It is

---

*This continues the reference to Jesus.

spiritual progress to live in the enthusiastic expectation of a child, in the love and wonder of a youth or a maiden, in the mature judgment of one who has lived longer; but through it all flowing is the eternal river whose source no man knows, because it flows from the heart of eternal love, friendship, compassion, appreciation. You can't do it unless you forgive yourself and everybody else. There is no hurt in love. "Perfect love casts out all fear"; there is nothing else left. There is no doubt in perfect love. So: to get over our sensitiveness and fear that people won't like us (which keeps them from it); to be without criticism in our minds (which irritates people whether anything is said or not); to flow along with life; to love and be nonresistant.

Now as I say, there are people who say this is silly. I've watched it, I've met them all—they have all been in my office, over and over again—and I have seen no person healed unless there came a time when he knew the Universe had no judgment against him or he against anyone else: he returned to the simple basis of the givingness of the Self, the recognition of the divine Presence in everything. If you and I want a friend, Emerson said, we must be one. We must love the world and be grateful and thank God for it; and we shall be happy because we shall be fulfilled. And that which we thought we did not have will be there in manifestation. This is not just a dream. Back of it there is a Law of Cause and Effect. Emerson called it "the High Chancellor of God," and Jesus said, "Heaven and earth will pass away, but my words shall not. . . . till all be fulfilled."

Think of the joy of it: that at last the harshness, the fear, the criticism, the doubt, the uncertainty . . . we may be fooled by a few people, but I'd rather be fooled by a few people than to completely fool myself about all people. I would rather believe in the instinctive integrity of the average person than to doubt it; and if we miss once in a while and don't ring the bell, think of the bells we *have* rung. And the Spirit isn't dried up and ossified and petrified. You go into an atmosphere where there is nothing but love, and the food will digest; there will be very little trouble or headaches; most diseases will automatically flow away as though they never belonged—because love is the only complete mental sanitation that there is. Just love. Just love.

And it is so simple and so dynamic. The practice of it also is simple. All truths are simple. There are only a few great fundamental laws in the Universe. Life gives; we must receive it. To fulfill the receipt of our gift, we must give it. That which goes out will come back multiplied and must go out again, and again and again. High motivating power, the deep spiritual inner awareness—that for which the heart longs and the mind yearns and the soul speaks—the Spirit already possesses.

O Love that will not let us go! And let's practice that love and that friendship, asking no man, "Is it intellectually sound? Can science prove it?" Science is an observer of the phenomena of nature, and that is all. They can kill the nightingale and not capture the song. Psychiatry is the Thing without a soul; and I believe it. But you and I are warm, colorful, pulsating human beings; the eternal Heart beats in our breast; even the Mind of God cries out through a great sage and says, "Come unto me all ye that labor and are heavy laden and I will give you rest. Take my yoke upon you, and learn of me; for I am meek and lowly in spirit. For my yoke is easy and my burden is light and ye shall find rest unto your souls."

O God, Thou who dost inhabit eternity and dwell in the innermost sanctuary of our hearts, we open our consciousness to the revelation and embrace of the Universe. O Love, as we receive, we give and we bless the gift; and we would know eternal sweetness, ineffable beauty. Thou God, who is Love: it is our desire that every person we touch shall be healed, every situation we enter shall be made whole. We would that our presence shall bring joy and peace; and so it shall. And so it is. Amen.

Let's give as we never gave before in our lives. The eternal Giver gives through us, and we give of ourselves and make it soar to a soul that is starving in darkness. Amen.

AFFIRMATIVE-PRAYER MEDITATION

(Now we have the names of people in this box, and they are going to believe with us that each one is attached to a divine and spiritual Pattern of his real Self.)

The inner Self, the Spiritual Self, the God Self exists here and now and is flowing through every organ and action and function of his physical being. And we rejoice in this and we permit it to be so; and he expects it to be so because it *is* so.

We know that every person who has asked for direction, wise counsel, receives it; everyone who has asked for greater success in life, or love, receives it. With him we accept the gift of Heaven from the God of Love and Peace and Joy. And so it is.

Now as we turn to that divine Presence which is both God and Man, we receive the beneficence of His love, the outflowing of His Spirit. And as we turn to each other, we bless each other and make the God of Love be—and abide—with us forevermore. Amen.

CHAPTER 13

How to Use a Power Greater than You Are

GOOD MORNING. I love you very much; and I guess you guessed that. I understand it has been real warm in Los Angeles. We have been in Monterey, and it has been wonderful and cool and a very wonderful convention. I was particularly impressed with the young people's work. One of my age likes to companion with people of the same age, so I spent a lot of time with these kids, and they are terrific. They had a healing peace meeting, and we were all so much impressed. It was a terrific thing, this consciousness, this knowing that the Universe in which we live is a little different than it looks.

Won't all of you take your program home and every day look at that building* and call it wonderful, praise it, and bless it, and know that when it is built, people are coming from all over the world and they are going to be healed and blessed; and that everything necessary to the most beautiful idea of a building is already there. I wish you would do that every day until it is completed.

*The prospective Founder's Church of Religious Science in Los Angeles.

It will be wonderful. The architect, Paul Williams, is a good metaphysician.

I think this audience is wonderful. I watched, and everyone comes smiling; and as they came in, I mentally hugged them, because I like people so much. And I thought, How wonderful! What a tribute to the Truth! And I said, "Maybe they all came to hear me; and if they did, then God is good to me." And *you* are good to me, and I love it and appreciate it.

Now we are talking on How to Use a Power Greater than You Are. We are talking about a spiritual Power everybody can use, if he believes in it and uses it. First of all, we say you could use a Power greater than you are spiritually; and someone will say, "Oh, what nonsense!" But let them stop to think a moment. Every time you plant a garden, you use a Power greater than you are. No one living knows how to make an oak tree. There isn't anyone living knows how an egg gets into a hen or how a chicken gets out of the egg; or how the chicken gets in the egg or how the egg gets out of the hen. All the scientific minds—and I believe completely in science—do not know how you can eat cheese and crackers and everything else.

We are three-dimensional people living in a four-dimensional world. They have proven at Duke University, in ESP, that we can reproduce the activities of the five physical senses without using the organs of the senses. They have proven we can think without the brain. (It will prove very helpful to many of us, I am sure.) They have proven theoretically that you can get along without this body and still be you.

No one has ever seen some other person. We *feel* him.

211

No one ever saw love or life or truth or beauty. Yet they are there. We are three-dimensional beings living in a four-dimensional world which governs the three dimensions. In the hen somewhere is the egg, in the egg somewhere is the chicken. We do not have to try to explain the inexplicable. That is why Jesus said that the Kingdom of Heaven is like a child: "Suffer the little children to come unto me and forbid them not, for of such is the Kingdom of Heaven." A *childlike* mind doesn't mean *childish*—just simple, *child*-like, and believing.

There is a Power in the Universe greater than we are. There is an Intelligence acting as Law that receives the impress of our thoughts as we think them. It is creative, and It always tends to create for us the conditions we think about and accept; and if we wish to help someone else, when we identify the person we wish to help with what we call our treatment or meditation, it will be for that person.

Somebody might say, "I don't believe it." Well, I don't care; it is none of my business. Somebody might say, "It is ridiculous!" That doesn't bother me any. The first steam-driven boat that crossed the Atlantic carried on it a scientific treatise on why it couldn't be done. We don't have to worry about whether somebody believes it. Who cares? Our only concern should be do we *know* what *we* believe. Are we *certain* of what we believe; can we *prove* what we believe, *demonstrate* it. And we *can*. And that is that.

Now I don't think it should seem strange. Somebody might say, "Why didn't the Bible tell us about it?" Maybe it did and maybe it didn't. Why didn't the Bible tell us about automobiles? Because it just didn't. You don't have to say it had to be in the Bible to be correct; very little we have nowadays was in the Bible. Somebody might have said, "If God had intended it to be that way, He would have revealed it some way." God didn't reveal *anything* until we were ready to take it. Look at modern science. Somebody thinks about it, specializes on it, dwells on it mentally until finally he discovers the secret. The secret of prayer we are going to talk about next week —they have proven it in Redlands in a university.

It has nothing to do with whether you are a Catholic, or a Protestant, or a Christian Scientist, or even a Religious Scientist. Whatever this thing is, it is no respecter of persons. It likes everybody. Everybody can go and climb up in the lap of God and whisper in His ear and get patted on his head and hear Him say, "You are My nice little boy"; and I believe that. God is personal to everyone who personifies God; God is as good to us as we are good to God; God is as colorful as we are colorful. God, infinite Peace, delivers that Peace to us at the level that we gain peace, and Love only knows and comprehendeth love.

If anyone who thinks he has love in his life knew how to surrender himself to Love, he would be the most amazed person in the world; and if somebody else says it isn't true, he wouldn't even know they are talking! *There is a Power greater than you are, and you can use It.* I can't explain why It is there—why is life?—nobody can. I do not believe that Power knows any more about Christians than It does Jews, or Jews than It does Gentiles; It knows nothing about our little idiosyncrasies, thank

God. Tennyson said, "Our little systems have their day; / They have their day and cease to be; / They are but broken lights of Thee, / And Thou, O Lord, art more than they."

You see? Simple, childlike minds, having faith, believing, accepting that there is a Power greater than we are and that we can use it—for what purpose? Every purpose. People sometimes say to me, "Well, is it spiritual to pray for, or use the power for, material things?" There is no such thing as a material universe. Science has long ago dissolved a material universe (as though there were a universe separate from the Truth that governs it and moulds it). There isn't anybody today who believes in that kind of a material universe.

There is a Power greater than we are, and everything that is visible is hitched to It—an invisible Pattern, a divine Pattern. All things come forth from It, and all things return again to It; and we are in It, and It responds directly to us personally at the level of our conviction that It is responding. And somebody might say, "Why doesn't It *force* it on us?" It doesn't force anything on anyone. We might say, "Why doesn't the garden grow carrots when we planted the beets?" When you plant a beet seed, the ground will say "beets," and when you plant a potato, it will say "potatoes." It will not say, "I don't like beets or potatoes." It's kind after kind. Someone will say, "Well, is it good to use the spiritual for our human needs?" I don't see anything wrong with it; we are trying all the time. Now I have friends who are good, honest vegetarians—yet they wear leather shoes. Shakespeare said, "Consistency is a jewel seldom worn"; and I have often facetiously said, "You won't eat meat, yet you wear leather shoes. Do you find it easier on the animal to skin it alive?" It is like the man who was so kind he didn't want to hurt a dog when he cut its tail off, so he cut it off a joint at a time.

Does the Universe want us to have *succotash*? Does it say, "I refuse to grow *lemons*"? Of course not. We have been so afraid of God, thinking we are made to suffer here so we will suffer less hereafter—or more—that we are all screwed up in our simple ideas about our relationship to the Infinite. Isn't it funny that we do not have a more close and intimate sense of relationship that there couldn't be any God in the Universe that withheld anything from us—? But there are certain laws we have to obey when we use the laws of Nature, and it is the same in the spiritual world as it is in the physical—because the spiritual just reproduces the physical on a higher level. The laws work just the same.

For instance, there is a law of attraction and repulsion in Mind; it works just like attraction and repulsion in physics; it always tends to bring to us that which is like our own thinking. All energy returns to its source. Einstein even has said that time, light, and space bend back upon themselves. Therefore our word tends to come back to us. "Whatsoever things are lovely and of good report—*think* on *these* things," the Bible says. "As a man thinketh in his heart, so is he." "Believe and it shall be done unto you."

There is a Principle that responds to us: this is the secret. There is a mathematical mental Principle that responds creatively to us at the level of our own consciousness. To the pure in heart all will be pure. To the ones who see that everything is wrong, everything will be wrong. To the ones who criticize everyone and everybody, they will always find something to criticize, and they will gradually get so mean that their best friends will walk away from them after they get tired listening to it.

But we know what it is: they are trying to justify themselves—they are afraid of themselves, they don't believe in themselves, they have a sense of guilt and rejection and an anxiety and insecurity within themselves; therefore they are sick. In this sense, we should be sorry for them; but there is no reason why you and I should have to spend a whole day with somebody who is mean. *I* won't. I just don't like it. I like beauty and laughter and song and dancing and fun. There is no reason to suppose that God is some sad creature sending thunderbolts to Methodists and candy to Baptists. I believe one is as good as the other, and a heretic is as good as someone who is not a heretic—but he might (or might not) have misssed something; it doesn't matter. The Universe loves all of us; It is impartial. That is why Jesus said, "He causes His sun and rain to come alike on the just and on the unjust."

Yes, there is nothing in nature or in God that withholds our good from us. Jesus said, "I am come that ye might have life and that ye might have it more abundantly"; so that's that. There is nothing in the Universe that keeps us waiting until we get saved. I understand there are certain people who are saved. I haven't met them. I understand there are certain people who are not saved. I haven't met them either. I never met "them" that you hear so much about. Where are "they"? *Who* are "they"? People come and say, "Ernest—you shouldn't do this; they don't like it!" And I always say, "*Who* don't like it?" "They." And I say, "Bring one of 'them' to me and I will explain why I am such a nice guy." But if "they" are so elusive, we can never get a hold of them.

I am not afraid of "them." Not at all.

Every man has to do the best he can. "To thine own self be true; and it shall follow as the night the day, thou canst not then be false to any man." You and I believe in a Power greater than we are. We believe It is Good; we believe It is Love; we believe It is Truth; we believe It is Beauty; we believe It responds to us; and we believe if we maintain a certain mental attitude of thought, It will automatically bring to us those things that make life happy. And we believe life ought to be happy. There is no "weeping God"—of this I am sure.

Emerson said, when his beloved son died, for two years he wept and sorrowed and grieved, until out of the weeping and the sorrow and the grief he learned how empty it was, how useless. And that is true. It seems as though Life, acting as Law, is quite impersonal.

You and I believe in something so stupendous and yet so simple. Its simplicity is what eludes us. If I can get all the thoughts out of my mind that say to me "I am hurt; I am sensitive; my friends hurt me" without being mean about it, without being arrogant (signs that we are protesting too loudly and fighting back), and if it is *real*: finally nothing in the Universe will hurt me, and finally I shall not any longer be led into situations where people will even wish to—and they can't.

This Thing is personal to you and to me, just as is all that God has and is and all the laws of the Universe. Isn't all of the law of electricity at the point where any electrician uses it? Isn't all the law of mathematics and higher calculus right at the fingertips of the mathematician when he is using a pen or pencil? Isn't all the harmony there is flowing through the one who sings, and all the beauty through the artist? *All* of it—? Well, of course! All of gravity is holding everything in place, as though all of gravity devoted its entire time to holding a peanut right there, if I put it there.

Now this is terrific. Someone said, "Go not thou in search of Him / But to thy self repair. / Wait thou within the silence dim, / And thou shalt find Him there." God we meet in ourselves and in each other and in Nature and everywhere. But how can we meet a God of love if we are looking at a life of hate? It isn't that way! And *Love* is not withholding. How can we meet a God of abundance if we are looking at impoverishment? Now I am not saying it is easy—but I do say it is *simple*. I say it is *very* simple. How can we look at, or see, or experience, a God or a life of harmony if we are always in discord?

But do you know, there is a certain psychological morbidity about all of us. I have known men and women who really love each other who periodically kick each other's teeth out so they can make up again. This is very common. It is one of the morbid traits of the human mind. And in that background is the idea that we suffer all this world and then go to a good place after; but those who disagree with us: the elevator goes down— way down!

That isn't so. The Universe comes fresh, new, clean, beautiful, lovely, exuberant, "exhilarant," majestic, dynamic, omnipotent to each one of us every moment of our time—That which is the original creative Energy and Force and Intelligence; That which is alive with life and aflame with love, right at the point of our listening, right at the point of our seeing, right at the point of our hearing. "Eyes have they but they see not, ears have they but they hear not, tongues have they"—but they speak no language of infinite Harmony and Peace.

Now this is the way it is. We didn't make it that way, but thank God that *is* the way it is, and thank God that each one of us has access to the infinite and ineffable All. We have to believe this. Someone may say, "*I* can't believe it." Then I am sorry; I wish you could. *I* think It is true. Someone may say, "It is ridiculous." Well, I'm sorry you think it is ridiculous; I wish you thought it was as simple as planting sunflower seeds and getting sunflowers. Did you ever hear of any creative soil that, when you plant sunflower seeds, will give you potatoes? Jesus understood this. Kind for kind. Somebody might say, "I want to be unhappy and have happiness come to me." I'm sorry: it isn't that way. You jump over a cliff, you are going to fall; and gravitational force isn't mean because it gets you there. And the trouble isn't the falling, anyway; it is the *landing*—quick, when you land! That is really where the disaster starts: at the bottom of the cliff.

You see, when we get to spiritual things, we get kind of woozy. We don't expect the laws of Nature to disobey themselves to please the naturalist. No one does. Somehow it is a peculiar thing: when we come to mental, psychological, and spiritual things, we expect the whole order of the Universe to reverse itself and chaos and confusion to take the place of law and order. But it doesn't.

It is fundamental to this whole thing that we must learn to affirm what we desire; we must learn to enthusiastically expect these things we desire. And as we advance in demonstration of this most fascinating of all sciences

. . . because it is a science, the Science of Mind—just as much a science as the science of electricity. After a while we are going to learn what Parker* and these people down here proved: that the prayer works, no matter how simple, no matter whether Jew or Gentile prayed it—a boy right off the football field; they didn't care. They said, If it works, it works; and if it doesn't, it doesn't; and if it *does*, it is a principle; and if it is a principle, it *will*. And it did. Isn't that wonderful—the Affirmative Prayer I want to talk about next week. *Everybody* can pray.

Everybody can pray an affirmative prayer; so don't be afraid as to whether or not this Power greater than you are is going to operate for you. *It can't help it.* It acts by reflection. Now we will imagine there is a mirror back there; it isn't a mirror: it is really a camouflage—a pretense, but pretty. I hold up my hand and see my fingers mirrored down there. Now suppose we go down there —let's say that it *is* a mirror—and try to scratch it out of the mirror, or rub it out: you can't do it. It is there just the same.

Suppose, then, I finally discover it is my hand that makes the reflection, and I say, "But I can't move my hand!" That is the position we are in now: we believe in the reflection. But I gradually find if I withdraw my hand and put something else out there, *that* is reflected. Then I am on the pathway to the greatest discovery of my life: that you don't have to change the *reflection*. That is the outside condition—it didn't make itself. All you have to do is change the imagery, which didn't make itself. *You*

*Dr. William Parker, researching the power of prayer at Redlands University.

made it, and *I* made it, and *we* are the creators and arbiters of fate. There is no law under the one great Law of Life but our own soul shall set it, as it obeys that great Law of Life.

Then you have to experiment with it. No use in our coming every Sunday and talking about these wonderful things and doing nothing about them. Work it during the week. Make yourself *let* it work the only way it *can* work, and that is to *convince yourself.*

Now the next thing to remember is this: you and I carry around the thought-habit patterns of the ages (this is well known in psychology), endlessly repeating them. "Man is born to be unhappy, to be sick and poor and to get dead," and some say to go up and some say to go down (I believe, *to go over into a broader territory,* and, I believe, *never to come back;* but it doesn't matter). We are here now, and the things our ancestors believed, be they right or wrong, operate through us—so much so that when somebody first said the world was round, they said he was crazy. When somebody first announced gravitational force, they said *he* was crazy. When somebody first announced the blood circulated, they said *he* was crazy. And the Spanish Inquisition was based on a theology which was sincere but believed it had to put on the rack those who disagreed with it. Galileo was made to recant, but I understand when he got up from his knees he said, "The darned thing is true just the same!" He knew it didn't matter what the other gentlemen had in mind. They were ecclesiastical sadists.

You in the integrity of your own mind, in the simplicity of your own thought, in the directness and childlikeness of your own heart. That is why Jesus said, "If you

221

ask your parent for a fish, will he give you a stone, or for an egg a scorpion? How much more shall your heavenly Father give you those things which are good." This is the way the heavenly Father gives it: through the Law of asking and receiving—the Law of the Power greater than we are receiving the impress of our thoughts and acting upon it.

Since we all carry these deep-rooted thought patterns, they are automatically projecting perhaps a destiny we do not like, and we say, "Can that be the result of my own thought?" Not the result of your own personal thought, I don't believe—but the result of the sum total of *all* thinking, operating through all of us. I don't like to pick out myself or someone else and say, "Oh well, Nature is beating you up because you are no good." I don't believe in that. We are all struggling for the Light. "But what am I? / An infant crying in the night; / An infant crying for the light; / And with no language but a cry." "But the feeble hands and helpless, / Groping blindly in the darkness, / Touched God's right hand in that darkness / And are lifted up and strengthened."

You may be sure of this: there is an integrity to your soul such as you will find nowhere else in the Universe. Here you will meet life; here you will decide; and here you may neutralize the thought patterns of the ages by simply denying them—and saying something greater than that (and I believe in it): "There is a Power greater than I am, and I accept It." And no matter what the mistakes are, the Universe holds nothing against us, ever. "He took my book all stained and spotted, / And gave me a new one, all unblotted, / And into my sad eyes smiled, / 'Do better now, my child.' / Should not the judge of all the earth do that?"

Shall not the Giver of all life eternally give? Shall not That which is Love forever hold us in Its embrace? Now at last we have learned our cooperation with It as we have in every other thing in life—because even Love acts as Law. Our part is really to wipe the slate of the past clean from fear and doubt and unloveliness and write a song on it and draw children playing on the shore, happy, naked, and unafraid; and then to know that *we* are that child, *we* are that person, *we* are that beloved of the Eternal God—we in the simplicity of our integrity, in the childlikeness even of our ignorance, because we are all ignorant. Each may say to himself, "The Eternal God is my refuge; underneath are the everlasing arms."

You will prove it all alone to yourself, my sweet and beloved friends; each will have to prove it to himself and for himself. Others can heal us and cure us and help us—that is good. But the *long* healing, the *deep* healing —that which shall be with us from now on, thank God— each can and must do for himself; and then he knows something new happens to him. He lives in a different universe. He is no longer afraid of the present nor morbid over the past, nor insecure over the future; but looking up and out, he sees God's divinely intended Man, God's beautiful Creation, and the strength of the hills are his and the beauty of the early morning sunrise and the softness of the sunset, the cool river in which he plunges —all around there is infinite and ineffable Beauty; and he knows that he is the beloved of God.

223

AFFIRMATIVE-PRAYER MEDITATION

(Now we are going to practice what we have been talking about. There are many names in this box; most of these people are in this audience or they have asked for someone. There is someone here who knows what each of these requests is—personal for someone else. Will you, then, as the rest of us think about this, believe that it is now done. Always accept the affirmative, but don't work too hard at it. I mean don't say, "It is done" questioningly. You see, when we get all worked up about it, we don't believe it and we are trying to scream down the negation. Resist not evil and it will flee from you.)

So we turn within and we are speaking about the name of all who have asked for physical healing. God is within each one of them—perfect Life is in each one of them—a divine Pattern of perfection is within each one of them. Every organ and every action and every function of this physical body is governed by divine Intelligence in each one of them; there is perfect circulation, perfect assimilation, and perfect elimination. There is one Life, that Life is perfect, that Life is their life. All the enthusiasm that there is, all the energy and action that there is in the Universe, is flowing through them. They sleep in peace and wake in joy and live in a consciousness of God, of good, of wholeness. Our word is the law of elimination to everything that denies this. We affirm that perfection, we announce their perfection;

we rejoice in it and we are glad. We know our word goes on until all is accomplished.

(Now everyone who has asked for betterment in circumstances or guidance knows his name or the one he has asked for. Let him believe he has received what he has asked for; and you and I will know, and we are so happy to announce, that he is governed and guided and directed by divine Intelligence.)

Everyone here who has asked for that shall always know what to do and how to do it and where to go and how to get there. He shall be surrounded by love and friendship. And there is nothing in him that can deny good, abundance, plenty—everything that makes life worthwhile—better than he has ever asked for, more than he can think about, beyond the range of his present knowledge. That good is coming to him which he shall be compelled to recognize, see, and act upon. If it is necessary for him to make decisions, he will. He will act wherever he is supposed to act, he will do whatever he ought to do. Back of it all we feel drawing to him everything that is good and worthwhile.

Now we say for all of us here—each one of us says to himself and to each other—we are the beloved of God. No arrogance in this. Very simple. We live— therefore we must be the beloved of God; and we are recognizing that divine Presence as joy, as infinite peace, as beauty, as perfect health, as love and friendship; and we are saying the doorway of opportunity stands wide open before us. It has nothing to do with our education or color or age or our creed or our doctrine. All of these things are swept aside.

We are the beloved of God. We are that which Thou art, Thou art that which we are; and in the Secret Place of our heart—in the Secret Place of the Most High—we commingle with the Eternal; and it is our desire, and we shall accept it individually and as a group, that every person we meet shall be glad. Wherever our shadow is cast shall healing take place; everything we look at we shall embrace and love. We desire to heal every situation we contact, whether we are aware of it or not. And it is so. "Beloved, now are we the Sons of God."

Now may the eternal light of Heaven guide your pathway and mine; may the everlasting Love and Peace and Joy of Life be and abide with us, and may we so live and so give that everything we touch shall commingle with us in the divine offering of Life to Itself, in the joy of the living, and in a peace which is perfect. Amen.

CHAPTER 14

The Prayer That Gets Results

GOOD MORNING. I want to thank you again for being here, so many of you in the summer—it is a great tribute to the new idea which comes to the world through the name of Religious Science, which I think is the next great spiritual impulsion. I think in the next 25 years there will be thousands of Religious Science churches throughout the world. It is inevitable. It is the greatest intellectual and spiritual freedom that has ever come to the world since the time of Christ. It has terrific simplicity. I do appreciate your being here, more than I can tell you, or how much I love you. I have had people tell me my Sunday morning service was not dignified. I'm glad and like it this way when people clap. We don't have to be afraid to say, "Praise God!" because we believe there is no hell. We ought to scream it louder.

Our subject this morning is "The Prayer That Gets Results." All prayers probably have some effect; some prayers must have a *complete* effect. Jesus, was, in a certain sense, in his time a Reform Jew. He said, "When ye pray, believe that you have, and you will receive." I met a couple of kids out here this morning, each of them 16;

they are of a different race; but there is only one race in my mind, and that is the human race—we all belong to it, just like there is only one God—and I embrace everyone alike and love everyone exactly alike. What God has made alike, we cannot separate.

One of these boys said he was going to be an engineer, the other said he wanted to play football. Perhaps neither one of those kids ever heard what I am going to talk about; probably I will never see either one of them again; but listen, guys, and use it and prove it to yourself, because if you use it the way I am going to talk about, it will work: affirmative prayer. They discovered, as you will see in this book—*Prayer Can Change Your Life**— at Redlands University, that when people prayed affirmatively, as it is done now, they got 70 percent better results than by the ordinary prayer, no matter how fervent.

Now you will find *why* in *this* little book that only costs $1.00; but you ought to have both of them. I like the book out of a university that comes to us and says, "We, without respect of creed, color, education have proven they can pray affirmatively and get results." But they have not explained *why*, and I am going to explain why this morning. They have *proven* it: that is the most valuable piece of spiritual information, in my estimation, that ever came from a university in the entire history of the educational development of the world—a university, impartial, impersonal. They didn't ask, "What church do you belong to?" or "Do you belong to any?" They just said, "Come and let's try it"—and that is good. And they

*By William Parker and Elaine St. Johns.

found a 70 percent better result when you pray affirmatively. You and I want to know *why*.

I will tell you why, I think, and it is very simple. You see, if prayer is answered at all—and it is—then theoretically all prayers ought to be answered. There is no God who loves one type of religionist better than another, and I don't believe there is a God who knows one race or creed is better than another, or a Jew better than a Gentile; I don't think there is any God worried about our little idiosyncrasies. Tennyson said "Our little systems have their day; / They have their day and cease to be; / They are but broken lights of Thee, / While Thou, O God, art more than they." Jesus answered it when he said, "When ye pray, BELIEVE THAT YOU HAVE." In other words, what Jesus said—what the modern metaphysical movements have proved, what they have proved in the last few years in the Redlands University, and what you and I have already accepted but may not know well enough or I wouldn't be talking about it—is that prayers that are answered are prayers that are affirmative and are accepted by the one praying.

I am going back in October to visit a school for boys that is independently run, where these boys from the age of 10 to 18 are taught to pray for what the school needs —and they make what we call demonstrations. They are taught to pray and believe it, and all get together and pray. Not long ago they prayed for a gym and someone came along and built it for them.

There is a definite record of a man who had a school in Boston years ago called The Cullis, I believe. He was so advanced in the technique of prayer that he always prayed alone for what he wanted, and he wouldn't let people be in his employ who doubted. He said if they doubted God for 15 minutes, they couldn't be there. I am afraid if we disposed of everybody who doubted God for 15 minutes we would be left in "splendid isolation." But this man got results.

He was going to the harbor at Halifax one time—this isn't a weird fish story, this is true and on record—and there was a heavy fog, and he told the captain, "I will have to go below and pray," and he did. And when he came back on deck, the fog had cleared away and the captain said, "This is a miracle and can't happen—but it did!"

We must believe there is a Power greater than we are, to begin with. Whether you call it God or divine Principle—I don't care what you call it. There is Something around us that receives the impress of our thought and reacts to it the way we think it. Mrs. Wilcox* said, "For life is a mirror of king and slave, / Tis just what you are and do; / Then give to the world the best that you have, / And the best will come back to you."

Now there is a divine Principle, a divine Intelligence, a universal Mind, a "universal Subjectivity," as Troward† called it. It doesn't matter what you call it—we are surrounded by some kind of a Law of Mind. Now God is beyond this Law, just as an electrician is beyond electricity. We are surrounded by a divine Presence and a universal Law.

---

*Ella Wheeler Wilcox (1850–1919), American journalist and poet, student of Emma Curtis Hopkins.
†Thomas Troward (1847–1916), English jurist, metaphysician, and author.

I am talking about the Law right now. It receives the impress of our thought; it is creative, it is intelligent, it acts upon it and tends to bring back into our experience that which we affirm in it. But remember this: if you can sit down once in a while and pray affirmatively and get a result, then what is happening *all* the time we think? Isn't that some kind of a prayer? If I say, "My poor head, my poor heart"—isn't that a prayer?

Now affirmative prayer—prayer that gets results—is one that believes in itself. We are surrounded by a Principle, a Law, an Intelligence, a Mind, a Creativity that receives the impress of our thoughts. I met this very sweet person in Florida last February—woman about 60—and I thought she looked so vital and rather pretty. She said, "I want to tell you something: a year ago I was a hopeless cripple, arthritic, could hardly walk, hands were knotted, every joint in my body ached"; and I said, "What happened?" "Well," she said, "I tried everything— even your practitioners—and didn't get much help"; and I said, "How did you do it?" She said, "I did it myself"; and I asked, "What did you do?" She said, "I just made up my mind there is an intelligent Principle everywhere and It flows through me and I can talk to It, and I began to praise It and began to tell every joint in my body what I wanted it to do and how wonderful I thought it was." And she said, "*This* is what happened!"

David Seabury,* the most popular lecturer on psychology—a friend of mine—told me that many years ago he had so much trouble with his stomach that it was terrible,

*(1885–1960), psychologist; son of Julius and Annetta (nee Seabury) Dresser, students and partisans of P.P. Quimby, mental healer and the "Father of New Thought."

and he tried the same thing: he began to talk to Intelligence there and told what he wanted It to do, and he got all over it. Now this is merely to show there is an intelligent Principle that runs through everything; and in experimenting, we ought to try everything and see what works. One of the prophets in the Old Testament said, "Try me herewith, saith the Lord, and see if I will not open to you the windows of Heaven and pour out such a blessing you will not be able to receive it."

There is an Intelligence that responds to us; but everything we think is some kind of a prayer, isn't it? We say, "I will sit down and meditate," and that is good; but unless in doing it we change our thought, there is no use doing it. There is no use sitting down for ten minutes and saying, "I am surrounded by prosperity; everything I do shall prosper," and the rest of the 24 hours saying "Nothing is any good." These are the moments when we center our thinking; we learn to accept. First of all, remember there is a Power greater than we are which reacts, a Principle that responds. It has now been proven—not only in religious experience in modern metaphysical movements such as ours (they are built up on this). That is why you are here—because something new is happening in the world, and this is it.

There is Something that responds. Now we have established this. Don't be impatient because of Its utmost simplicity; let's grasp It. But let's get the basis sound, and let's get it mathematical. We are thinking centers in a universal Mind that receives the impress of our thought and acts upon it, and reacts to it according to our affirmation. If this can be proven in a university, it certainly should be better proven in the church, where they arealdy believe in these powers. If this is so, we have established a Principle. Now they didn't do this at the university. They pointed to a *fact*. I said to Elaine,* I hope the next book you write, you will establish a *Principle*, and I would like to talk with you about it.

What they have done proves the truth of what I am talking about. It is the most feasible explanation as to why any prayers were ever answered. You see, it didn't matter what their religion was. If they prayed believing, they got a result. Since we know this, let's do it consciously and definitely and knowing what we are doing. There is a Principle that returns to us, therefore It responds by corresponding or reflection. This is why Jesus said, "When ye pray, believe that it is done."

Now that is the simple basis: there is a Power that responds creatively—It can't help it—and apparently It responds mathematically. The whole Universe seems to operate mathematically, because It is the Cosmos—It is intelligent. Therefore we personally and individually should be able to decide what the response is going to be. That is the next thing we have to establish. Sometimes people say to me, "I read a great tirade in a magazine lately where people more orthodox than we said it was a shame the way people were coming to our movements —not only Religious Science, but all the New Thought movements—because they were promised so much."

We believe Heaven is *now*; God is *now*. There will never be a day in eternity better than the day in which you and I are living, or any different. It is a continuity.

*Elaine St. Johns, co-author of *Prayer Can Change Your Life*.

Without criticizing them, let us say that what they hope to get later, we would like to have now and keep later. We do not wish to deny others the privilege of entering into Heaven some day and enjoying these things which now they do not have. I merely say we believe it ought to be possible to have them now and keep them. There is nothing wrong with it.

Now it was not difficult for Jesus to pray effectively. It was not hard for this man to pray so he always got an answer, because he wouldn't keep any man close to him who doubted for 15 minutes. He said, "I cannot have anyone so close to me who doubts God." I don't care how orthodox he was—he had cleared his mind so he knew God would answer him, and that was that. After that is established—a Power greater than we are—It responds by corresponding. We approach It affirmatively; and when we pray, we say, *"It is so."* "When ye pray, believe that ye have." This is fulfilling it.

Now the next thing I want to consider is the *degree* of fulfillment; because even in our field we find some people are better practitioners than others. I don't mean they are better people; I don't mean they are more sincere. But they have what we call a greater consciousness. I measure everything in our work with a measuring rod of *consciousness* and nothing else; that is, the inner feeling and acceptance of a person. The inner mental reaction.

I have seen kids who had this consciousness; old people; young people. It has nothing to do with race, color, creed; nothing to do with intellectual attainment; nothing to do with your I.Q. as it is measured in schools. It has to do only with—*Do you have the capacity to believe?* and *Are you using your belief at a certain level of consciousness?* I think this is important.

I do know that in our field certain people do better than others. Some people treat more effectually for some things. I have known people who were better at physical healings and others who were better at finances or affairs. The only reason is in their own mind. I have noticed, and this should be revealing, that if people have had a very good background of success before they come into our work, it is easier for them to succeed, because they are merely applying what they already have to a new medium. It is like a salesman. A man who is a good salesman will be a good salesman with whatever he sells as soon as he learns the nature of his product.

It is like a good religion: everyone is just as "fervent"; but some might be better in consciousness, religiously. It doesn't matter what they believe outside; it is what they do to themselves inside that we are talking about. We are merely a group of people who happen to understand there is a Principle governing this, and this is the way it works, and we have a technique for using it. Use it this way, and you will get a result; and *everybody* in our field should get a result.

I have noticed that the people who have the greatest awareness of God can pray most effectively—but they still have to pray affirmatively. They pray effectually, but they pray affirmatively. For instance, you take a man who has a great consciousness of peace. He isn't afraid of anything; his calm trust of God is complete. He knows the Universe is not against him, It is for him. And he is working for, treating for, or praying for a discordant condition where there is very little peace. Hasn't he got more peace as a background for his affirmation than someone who is confused? That is all I mean. *He has.* His prayer will be more effective, even though it will still follow the

law of *all* prayer: it is done unto you as you believe. You
have to believe first. Action and reaction.

Now just because it *is* action and reaction, certain
actions will produce certain reactions. The higher the
action, the higher the reaction. One thing I thank God
for in life more than anything else: I have never had to
go through much fear in my life. I have gone through
trouble, chagrin, sadness; not much pain and almost no
fear, because my mother brought us up without fear but
very religious—that is, we read the Bible every day, said
Grace at every meal, got down on our knees and said
family prayers at night. But we were Congregationalists;
and they are very liberal. She didn't want us to be scared
to death; and I was grown up and away from home
before I knew grown-up, adult people actually believed
in a hell and a devil; and I don't know *now* how they
can—because I haven't the mental equivalent. I was
brought up that way, and that is a great heritage. And it
is worth more than millions of dollars.

Someone who isn't afraid ought to be able to heal
somebody who is, and following the same Principle.
Therefore I say, this is the prayer that is bound to be
answered, it seems to me. This is only my opinion, and
I want you to try it. I do not know any more about these
things than you do—I just am not afraid to get up and
talk about them. It is a habit.

Very simple things you and I believe—very simple,
fundamental things. We are spiritual beings in a spiritual
Universe governed by laws of Intelligence. The Law of
Mind in action is the final law of the Universe. Modern
science is beginning to accept it; it has to be that way.
Therefore Something responds. Now we don't need to

worry about this. It will happen. Consequently, we are praising our environment. Are we saying, "O you wonderful heart, you perfect head, you good feet"? We *are* saying, "Life is for me and not against me. Everywhere I go things will be made perfect before me"—what you and I call a treatment; what are we treating in our own minds. You don't argue with God, you don't make Law be Law. It *is* Law; God *is* God. "I am the Lord, beside which there is none other."

Now the next thing in doing it is to keep from denying what we affirm; and this, I think, is tough. No one ever heard me say this is easy; I say it is *simple*. I don't think it is *easy* to control your thinking. A child can understand it—and I think kids use it better. I got such a thrill out of the kids at Asilomar: there is a lot they don't have to unlearn. They accept it as natural, they use it, they believe it—and it works. It is no respecter of persons. That is why Jesus said, "Suffer the little children to come unto me and forbid them not, for of such is the Kingdom of Heaven. And verily I say unto you, their angel faces do forevermore behold the face of My Father which is in Heaven."

And Heaven is within. Some prayers will be more effective than others; but all prayers, to be effective at all, must be affirmative. We must accept the answer to our own prayer; and when we understand why, we will—you will and I will. Therefore we don't worry about it any more.

I believe love is the greatest healing motivating power in the Universe, because love is givingness. I don't think you will have a good effectual prayer or preacher or practitioner or human being without great love. It is the only thing that unbinds the captive, penetrates the prison wall of obscurity, and sets the captive free from the prison of his own creation and his own undoing. Well, we have to *do* it; this is not an idle dream. I want those two boys to do it. They are young, only 16, and I'll probably never see them again; but I want them to do it. Because they haven't learned yet how "terrible" everything is; they haven't become disillusioned with life. They are full of hope, ambition, expectation, enthusiasm, zest.

You and I have to return to that same place and throw out all these things we have accumulated throughout the years of unbelief—get right back again to that simple spot in our own heart. It is normal to have faith, it is natural to believe in God, it is right to love people, it is good to praise everything—because hidden in everything there is a seed of Perfection. There is a divine creative Intelligence in the center of everything, from a blade of grass to an archangel. There is Something that responds to us everywhere we go.

A person who will take time enough to believe there is a Life within him that lighteth everyman's path with Light, the path of thousands . . . one who embraces everyone in his own mind will be embraced by all. Here is a law absolutely inviolate. Last and not least, the great experiment is in our own mind. Who shall hinder? Who shall say to us no? Here in the integrity of our own souls, in the simplicity of our own hearts, you and I can prove what the ages have longed for, lived for, and prayed for: that at last, though we did not know it and the world did not suspect it, Divinity has temporarily clothed itself in humanity.

One Heart beats in the Universe in perfect rhythm. One Mind thinks through us. One Law executes Itself in and around us. Heaven lies close about us—so close, so near, so sweet, so ineffable. O living Truth, O Beauty so perfect, O Love that cannot let us go—the Light that lighteth every man's path; let every thought of fear or doubt or misunderstanding flee from us forevermore. Lord God of Heaven and earth, within and around us: we accept, we believe, we announce; for we are that which Thou art, and Thou art that which we are. And right now we announce that the Kingdom of God is with us. Amen.

I wrote those words as an adaptation of the Lord's Prayer. It says, "Thou doest forgive us as we forgive. / The Kingdom will come when all that live / Thy will have done." In the Bible it says, "Thy kingdom come, thy will be done on earth as it is in heaven"—one of the old teachings which go way back to the Hermetic teaching, which said, "As above, so beneath; as below, so above." What is true on one plane is true on all—the within and the without—and it is really saying that the Kingdom of God on earth will come when, through a realization of God within, the *will* of that Kingdom is done. "And forgive us our debts *as* we forgive our debtors" is another statement of cause and effect, the mirror of life. "It is done unto you as you believe." "Thou forgivest our debts as others we free," this says. It is the only way it could be, because there is your action and reaction again.

Will you please practice these things. The theory is wonderful and sweet—and it is true. You will have to prove it. Just make every prayer affirmative. Say, *"This is the way it is,"* and try to feel the reality of it; and then when you give your treatment, forget it. It is in the Law of Mind in action, though you do it every day. Gradually you will see how it works; you will be amazed at what happens, and it will all be so simple.

AFFIRMATIVE-PRAYER MEDITATION

(Now let's do it for a good many people, who have put their names in the box, wishing help. We are going to help them now. It is a privilege.)

They are going to accept the help, they are going to affirm with us that there is one Life, that Life is God, that Life is their life right now, that Life circulates through them. There is perfect circulation, assimilation, elimination. They are spiritual beings right now. All the Power there is and all the Presence there is is flowing through them. There is only one heart in the Universe; It has perfect rhythm. There is only circulation represented in the bloodstream. In this One Life there is nothing but Good, and we know there is perfect elimination of everything that does not belong. Let us enjoy the perfect health of these people, knowing that through what we are doing now whatever seems to be wrong will be removed. And whoever asked for guidance will receive it. Divine Guidance belongs to everyone.

CHAPTER 15

God and Your Personality

IT HAS been a great privilege and pleasure to speak to you these ten weeks. Next Sunday, Bill* will be back. A Chinese philosopher once said, "O man, having the power to live, why will ye die?" Isn't it strange this make-believe that we go through that we are so intelligent, and so on—when all we have to do is *be ourselves*, and then we will be great; because God made us great. Anything that gets us away from greatness is merely a stumbling over our own feet. "The great are great to us only because we are on our knees. Let us arise."

Thank you for the wonderful support you have given me these past weeks, the wonderful attendance—this wonderful crowd here this warm morning. It is a sign we are interested in something dynamic and vital, and we are interested together, and we are building a great monument† to the greatest truth the world has ever known. I

*William Hornaday.
†This probably is a reference to the building of Founder's Church of Religious Science, in Los Angeles. The "edifice" referred to in the fifth paragraph is unmistakably Founder's.

would like you to know that you are taking part in building that which symbolizes the most liberated spiritual thought since Jesus graced this planet with his presence.

Jesus was a simple man who taught the greatest truth the world has ever known. He did not claim to be a messiah. He said, "Why callest thou me good? There is none good save one, which is God." When they mistook him for what he taught, he said, "It is expedient that I go away, that the Spirit of Truth shall awaken in you the meaning of what I have been telling you."Ever since then, the people have taken the teaching and surrounded it with high walls, which have closed out a great deal more landscape than they closed in. Whoever puts a high wall around his small estate will cut out the greater horizon.

It is a very interesting thing to me, because while I started this movement, I have no personal feeling about it at all. It is great and it is good and it is wise, because it depends upon the Wisdom of the ages. We have no Prophets. We are the most normal and natural spiritual group of people who ever lived, because we are not afraid of God or the Universe or each other or the future or destiny. We know that we are in the keeping of an Intelligence beyond ours; that to err is human, to forgive is divine; that "the finite alone has wrought and suffered, the Infinite lies stretched in smiling repose."

I would like to say to you this morning that every dollar you give to this edifice—and you should all give something—you are giving to the greatest spiritual cause the world has ever known since Jesus was here, and to the cause which he magnified. The individual life, sensing its personal relationship to the Universal, will give and bless that gift. The Bible says, "What is man that Thou art

mindful of him, or the Son of Man that Thou visitest him;
for Thou hast made him but little lower than the angels
and hast crowned him with glory and honor."

Our theosophical friends refer to the Mind that sleeps
in the mineral, waves in the grass and vegetable, wakes
to simple consciousness in the animal, self-consciousness in man, and to Cosmic Conscious in the upper hierarchies—which means there are gradations of unfoldment
or evolution from the lowest to the highest. Just as there
are beings below us in awareness, there must be beings
beyond us in awareness, forever. "Ever as the spiral grew,
he left the old house for the new."

Our subject this morning is God and Your Personality,
and I would like to spend a few minutes in a rather abstract discussion; so please don't be bored with it. I did
not make it up. I happen to believe in it. All the deepest
thinkers who have ever lived have believed in it. It is simply this: the Universe is a spiritual system which you and
I accept. It is a system governed by laws of Intelligence.
Intelligence acts as Law. That is what is back of our treatment. We are all in a process of evolution or unfoldment.
There is incarnated in every person and in every thing the
image of God, the nature of God, the possibility of God.

Jesus said, "I say that ye are Gods and every one of you
sons of the most High." This is the great claim that Jesus
made on the Universe. "Who hath seen me, hath seen the
Father"; yet "the Father is greater than I." "Believe I
am in the Father, and the Father in me; or else believe me
for the very works' sake." He claimed that if we could see
into the center of things, we should see God. "And seeing the multitude, he went up into the mount. And when
he was set, his disciples came unto him, and he opened

243

his mouth and taught them, saying, 'Blessed are the pure in heart for they shall see God.'" He meant *right here, right now*, this morning. As we look at each other, there would be a spiritual penetration which would see back of the camouflage, back of everything that appears, to the divine Center of our being, which is God, and God incarnated in each one of us in a unique way.

The central teaching of the ages around which even Christian theology revolves, but most theologians do not know it (and many of them do and believe it is true) is that God is incarnated within each one of us. We had nothing to do with it; that is the way it is. That is the nature of the Universe—and, uniquely, of each one of us; and we are asleep.

But as we gradually wake up, we wake up to what already exists in the Mind of God. And because we wake up to it, it appears to us—"As thou seest, that thou be'st." That is our whole philosophy, it is the philosophy of Jesus, Plato, Socrates, of all the deep spiritual thinkers. But it has a practical application, it has a utilitarian purpose. Jesus said, "It is not I but the Father who dwelleth in me, He doeth the works"; and yet he did not hesitate to say, "I am the authority of God. My word is the Presence and the Power and the Activity of the Living Spirit; and what I am, ye are also."

"Whatsoever things the Son seeth the Father do, that doeth the Son also, that the Father may be glorified in the Son." Now the teaching is that God, the creative Spirit, incarnates and then lets us alone. Everything in Nature proves this, everything in evolution does, everything in the advance of science. Solomon did not know about an automobile. David, who by the way had the first orchestra and wrote the music for it himself and directed it— David was a great man. But he didn't know anything about modern appliances or electricity. Now all these things existed and waited for somebody to recognize them. Wouldn't it be funny if that were true of *our own nature*? That would be funny indeed! I wrote somewhere: "O *within* all things; *around*; / Brahma, Light of Life divine, / Shatter all our days of dreaming, / Absorb our being into Thine. / Let the mind awake to Brahma / That it no more separate be, / That the life that seemed divided / Be not lost but found in Thee."

Every man has a direct inlet to God. Every man is God as that man. That is the thing I want to think about in this discussion. I don't want you to think I thought all these things up. I believe them. They are true. All the great major religious origins have followed them—all of them. The Greeks taught them in mythology; in all their many Gods and all the things that seemed pluralism, was this one central thought; Emerson refers to it when he says, "There is one mind common to all individual men." You and I do not have a mind separate from God. We do not have a body separate from the Universe. There is one Mind, and we use It; one Spirit in which we live and by which we live; and one Law, which responds creatively to us as we think.

Someone was saying just last night they didn't believe much in treatment because they didn't want to be influenced. I said, "You don't know anything about what you are talking about; you don't understand this philosophy at all. No one influences anybody in our philosophy; no one treats anyone personally in treatment. He is merely referring to the spiritual nature of the individual, which is perfect.

There is inside you and inside me a Perfect Man— I don't know what he looks like. Whitman said, "At the center of everything nestles the seed of perfection." The Bible says, "Awake thou that sleepest and arise from the dead, and Christ shall give thee life." Browning refers to it as a spark which a man may desecrate but never quite lose. Emerson said it seems as though when we entered this world we had taken a drink too strong for us: "We are gods on a debauch." Now they have all said it. And you and I happen to believe in it. God in us—the Living Spirit. We do not believe we are lost souls, some going up and some going down. If there is weather hotter than this, I don't want to go to it; and moreover, I am not going.

"Heaven is lost for an idea of harmony." Many of us are in hell often and will stay there till we get out; and nothing seems to extricate us but ourselves. We have to choose to do it. Every man is "a god though in the germ."

What is this personality? I believe back of this personality, this objective and mental entity, there is a spiritual double. Now let's not get confused. I am not talking about a dual personality, or a split personality. I am just saying I happen to believe that deep within myself and yourself there is another self, of which *this* self is a lower extension, a lesser extension. I believe there is a pattern of perfection in us, for us, about us, with us, around us, through us that we didn't put there. In the beginning God made man perfect, but "man has sought out many inventions."

I happen to believe you and I are spiritual beings on the pathway of an eternal progress, with certainty before us, around us, through us, behind us, and in us—and that, as Browning said, "I shall arrive as birds pursue their trackless path." We are going to get there. We are hell-bent for heaven. We can't help it. You and I do not believe in lost souls or any of this theological nonsense whatsoever. We are liberated from the fear and the superstition of the ages, and I wouldn't be here if I didn't know that. Nor would you. It is so. But it means perhaps more than even we have ever thought.

I often think to myself. I love to just sit and think— and did, yesterday, for several hours. Sometimes I *just sit*, of course, and that is even more relaxing. I was thinking, What a stupendous thing to try to tell anybody! Only to an audience such as ours could I even talk about it; other people would say that we are crazy to say that each one of us is a divine being right now and a perfect being right now and an exalted being right now: it doesn't *look* that way. I understand that; but it *is* that way. "Thou hast made us; Thine we are; and our hearts are restless till they find repose in Thee." The poet* said, "Out of the night that covers me, / Black as the Pit from pole to pole, / I thank whatever Gods there be / For my unconquerable soul. / It matters not how strait the gate, / How charged with punishments the scroll, / I am the master of my fate, / I am the captain of my soul."

Jesus said, "Destroy this body and I will raise up another like unto it"; and when they told him they had power to destroy him, he just laughed at them. Then he

*William Savage Landor (1775–1864), in "Invictus."

said, "There is a truth which, if you know it, will free you." That truth, if it is going to free us, must be an interior thing. We arrive at it by a perception of the relationship of this immediate self to the Universe, to God, and to each other.

We need never be afraid that the knowledge of the Truth will produce a psychological or emotional instability; it is only a knowledge of spiritual Truth that will produce a mental *stability*. Nothing else can. We are so tied up with, and so tied into, and so much a part of, the Universe in which we live that we cannot separate ourselves from it. But we have freedom, choice, and volition; and while we deny this, it is but partly revealed. "Now we see as through a glass darkly, but then face to face. Now we see in part; then shall we know even as we are known."

You see, we are already known by God—by the Spirit —as the spiritual entity which we are. Now wouldn't it be amazing if you and I were the potential of all the power, all the energy, all the action, all the will, all the volition that there is in the Universe—all the endless manifestations and all the Beauty and Peace and Power—? I believe this is true. There is a self not revealed—"That inner self that never tires, / Fed by the deep eternal fires, / Angel and guardian at the gate, / Master of death and king of fate." That is you and that is me. "Oh!" but we say; "this *myself*? No such exalted being can have anything to do with me! I am weak! I am sinful!"

All of this is true about every one of us. But there is another self; there is an inner self. There is a spiritual—I don't know that you would call it "double," but *exten-*

sion: there is a spiritual—Socrates called it his *Daemon*. By that he meant his real Spirit, his Self. It is the Thing with which, or in whom, Jesus was in continual connection. He called it the Father within him. "Our Father which art in Heaven, hallowed be Thy name": Jesus was not praying to an external God, but to a divine inner Presence which he knew to be the universal side of himself. We are all universal. This is what is back of all extrasensory perception, which has nothing to do with sending out thoughts; it is the immediate perception of the soul in a field of unitary wholeness, whose center is everywhere and whose circumference is nowhere.

We deal with one Mind, one Spirit, one Man, and one Universe—but each man a unique individualization of all that there is. "Speak to him, then, for he hears. / And spirit with Spirit shall meet. / Closer is He than breathing, / Nearer than hands and feet."

This is what all great composers, artists, creative people listen to. They may not know it; they may doubt it. It doesn't matter: that is what they listen to. That is what directs them. That is what is back of all creativity: the original Creator *in me*. That is why Emerson said that the mind that wrote history is the mind that must read it; that it can be interpreted only from the standpoint of this mind. This mind is God, the one Mind common to all men. That is why he said the Ancient of Days is in the latest invention; why Kipling said, "There are other ears behind these ears"; and Jesus said, "Who hath seen me hath seen God."

Jesus, Walt Whitman, and Emerson, so far as I know, were the three greatest individualists that ever lived. There is no conceit in this individualization. I mean there

249

is nothing psychologically "smart" about you or me because God made us. We haven't anything to brag about or write home about because God made each one of us different. We need not be afraid to affirm our divine Inheritance; we *ought* to affirm It. But while we deny It, It does not appear. There is That within each one of us, which could not but overcome every adverse situation, whatever it may be, could not but rise triumphant, while we are in this world, to a more complete dominion, a greater happiness, a deeper joy, a higher exaltation, a more complete inward peace that is perfect.

Now this is the meaning of our personality. It isn't this little funny-looking thing. That is all right; I love it; I love all of the things it does. They are silly, but what difference does that make? We don't need to be afraid of being silly. Watch children play; watch puppies and lambs and dogs and kittens: all Nature is glad—but man pulls a long face and is sad, merely because he is not acquainted with himself. We ought to believe in this. It is the basis of everything we do without conceit, without arrogance. "Who hath seen me hath seen the Father," or God. Without any psychological inflation at all, why couldn't we say, "Wonderful me!" The ancients taught their disciples to say, "Wonderful me! I am that which Thou art, Thou art that which I am."

You know, the whole purpose, the whole aim of man is to discover himself. Medicine does not pretend to heal anyone. All they do is to permit Something that *does* heal *to* heal—and that is good, and I believe in it. Surgery does not do anything other than aid Nature. Psychiatry doesn't pretend to create an Ego; it merely removes what denies the realization, and when that is removed—the psychological and physiological obstructions—That which is already perfect assumes Its own prerogatives and comes forth as Lazarus came forth from the grave. We are dead psychologically and physiologically—but not spiritually. We are only half alive physically and mentally—but we are never incomplete spiritually.

There is a Perfect Man back of our psychological and physiological ego. If we want a brilliant personality, we have to be aware of this Man. It isn't that we want to influence people. That is of no importance to me. I wouldn't cross the street to influence anybody or convince anybody or sell anybody anything—because "a man convinced against his will is of the same opinion still." But I can say this: any person who will listen long and deeply to that divine Reality within himself will become aware of It, and he will gradually be directed by It. And he will know—and nothing can dissuade him of this one sublime, supreme fact—that "there is more to a man than is contained between his head and his bootstraps"; that he is an immortal being, on the pathway of eternal self-expression; that there is no final question about the safety or validity of his soul. "Look unto me, and be ye saved, all the ends of the earth."

And every man who believes that God in him is what he is, without conceit, now calls on that divine Presence: "Be what I am!" Loose It; let It go; open the doors of the prison of the Self and free this imprisoned Splendor. And whether it is selling shoes or polishing automobiles or racing horses or singing a song or writing a hymn: they are all the same thing. Let the unwise try to divide the indivisible— don't *you* ever try to do it!

God is in the child at play. "Bless children playing on

251

the shore, / To them belong the Pipes of Pan. / The song of sea, the surf's uproar. . . ." Children; but *we* are afraid to make this great claim on God. Everyone says we are sinners and displease God. Remember this: the Universe exists for the delight of God, and *you* are the delight of God. Why not accept it? There is no arrogance in it. Every song that was ever written was written by the one Mind, slightly differentiated in the uniqueness of the individual writer. If we could keep our minds open to that, we would have divine Direction. Now think of the difference in living with yourself if you think you are poor, weak, sick, a lost soul, nobody loves you, you hate everybody, and nothing is good. That is an unfortunate attitude, and it is encouraged because people say, "Well, we *ought* to do this."

You cannot get conceited if you are dealing with God. "Thine is the kingdom and the power and the glory for ever and ever. Amen." No, you can't be conceited if you say, "God made me and I'll have to accept what God has done. God never makes mistakes. I shall have to accept that somewhere hid within the depths of myself is the God-intended Man. I shall have to accept the fact that as I recognize Him, He will recognize me; as I permit Him to take over, He will know what to do." This is the God that Jesus prayed to: our Father in our Heaven—my Father in my Heaven, your Father in your Heaven—the eternal God. "O Living Truth that shall endure / When all that seems shall suffer shock, / Arise . . . on the rock, / And make us pure."

The Man that God sees—and "as thou seest, that thou be'st"—the man that God knows: shall we know something different? Don't try to develop such a dynamic personality that people fall dead when they look at you. A man said to me one day, "I have something way ahead of your stuff"; and I said, "Thank God; it is bound to happen." I said, "What can you do?" He said, "I can go down the street and look at a man in the back of the neck and he will turn around." And I said, "*Who* does *what* to *which*?! What is all this nonsense?" We are not trying to develop one of these dynamic personalities that breathe fire. Such people bore me into insensibility. They are "children crying in the night and with no language but a cry."

However if somebody ever walks the streets of Los Angeles knowing what Jesus knew about himself, the paralyzed people will get up and follow him gladly. If anyone knows anything about the Light that is at the center of his being, it will light the pathway of everybody he touches. If anyone knows anything about the Love that is all-embracing, his arms will be around everyone in the world. It is all nonsense to say God is Love unless our arms are around people. It is all nonsense to say God is Peace unless there is a peace in our own consciousness that brings calm to everything. It is nonsense to say God is giving unless our hands are open that we may scatter on the four winds of Heaven the last atom of good we have ever received. It is all nonsense to say the Universe holds us in Its loving embrace while we dislike one single soul. As Emerson says, "It writes 'Thou Fool' on the forehead of a king."

We don't have to develop this terrific personality that knocks them over and with just a look slays them. Not

at all. But we have to get rid of our denunciation of ourselves, of our renunciation of ourselves, and our denunciation of others, and begin to live as though this were the
divine Man. "I am that which Thou art, Thou art that
which I am." There is a perfect Man, my dear, at the
center of your own being. There is a song ready to be
sung; there is an oval form ready to be sculpted into
a magnificent deity, uniquely presented; and "There is a
God goes with it and makes it soar / To a soul that was
starving in darkness before."

You are that Light and *you* are that Love and *you* are
that Redeemer. You are that Messiah; you are the only
saviour you will ever discover in all your travels. This is
the secret Socrates and Emerson and Plato and Jesus and
Whitman wrested from the Universe. This is the Secret of
the Ages, the Lost Word, the Key to the realization of the
Kingdom of Heaven, the entering of the Fifth Kingdom
of our evolution and this is what happens: just as when
you look in a mirror physically you see a physical image,
there is another kind of mirror—more creative—in Life,
which is a Mirror of Mind; and as we behold ourselves
in It, It beholds Itself in us. And beyond that is the eternal Presence, ever pressing, gently urging, weakly calling,
forever embracing.

We are in the arms of a Tenderness, we are in the atmosphere of a Sweetness, we are in the presence of a Light
far beyond our dreaming. And in that Light there is no
darkness; and as we take time to practice this Presence,
feel the depths of this Peace, see the magnificence of this
Light and this Life in each other, something awakens in
us and, in its turn, within those we meet and the environ-

ment which we habitate. And gradually we are lifted from the lower rung of our own elevation in this earth, our own evolution on this earth; and we shall live here and now in the Kingdom of God.

"Beloved, now are we the sons of God." Let us live as though this sonship were real. Somehow out of that which appears as darkness, out of that which appears as isolation, fear, and doubt, and the wasted years, and the dissolution of life—like a Phoenix rising from the ashes of a dead self, some glorious form shall emerge and we shall sing, "Holy, Holy, Holy, Lord God Almighty; Holy, Holy, Holy, Lord God within me."

O Living Presence, O Eternal Sweetness, ineffable Beauty: we recognize Thy Presence, our souls enveloped by Thee, O Living Truth, Rock of our Salvation, O All-Embracing arms of the Infinite Sweetness and Tenderness. Our Father in our Heaven, may our love reach embracing each other and the world, that forevermore we shall sing Holy, Holy, Holy, Lord God Almighty; Holy, Holy, Holy, Lord God within me.

AFFIRMATIVE-PRAYER MEDITATION

(We have names here in this box of those wishing help and we hold them in our own consciousness for a few moments.)

Let's do that, knowing that each name in here and each one who put his name in here does the same thing and he receives it. He is the divine Man we have been talking about. That divine Man is recognized and realized, and manifests now. There is a divine Pattern of his physical body forever in the Mind of God, perfect. There is success and happiness and joy in everything he does. We receive for him, and know for him, and he expects for himself, guidance, perfect healing, perfect Love, perfect Wisdom. And so it is.

Now as we turn to that divine Presence which is both God and Man, we recognize our being in each other—in the infinite pattern of eternal Perfection—and it is our will to bring life and joy to everyone we meet. And the eternal Spirit goes with us, and we with It, now and forevermore. Amen.